Lesson Plans for Teaching Resilience to Children

Lynne Namka

Talk, Trust and Feel Therapeutics
Tucson, Arizona

Also by Lynne Namka

The Doormat Syndrome
The Mad Family Gets Their Mads Out
How to Let Go of Your Mad Baggage
Avoiding Relapse: Catching Your Inner Con
A Gathering of Grandmothers: Words of
Wisdom from Women of Spirit and Power,
Good Bye Ouchies and Grouchies, Hello Happy Feelings: EFT for Kids of All Ages
Teaching Emotional Intelligence to Children: Fifty Fun Activities
Parents Fight Parents Make Up: Take Good Care of Yourself
The Case of the Prickly Feelings

Fiction
The Starseed Child
Love as a Fine Species of Madness
Castalia Every After
The Loathsome Lady

The catalog for my books and curriculums is at www.AngriesOut.com
Downloadable pdf books are available at timetoloveyourself.com

Artwork by Marvin Alonso, Robert Silverstein, Jack Tone, PYRRTH,
Andreea Mironiuc, monkeysinmyhead and marvelhead.
Graphic clip art © Dianne J Hook. http://www.djinkers.com/home.php

Published by
Talk, Trust & Feel Therapeutics
5398 Golder Ranch Road
Tucson, Arizona 85739
lnamka158@earthlink.net

www.AngriesOut.com
www.HappyHealthyLoving.com
www.Nardar.com
www.timetoloveyourself.com

Dedicated to Martin Seligman and Carol Dweck
whose work on learned helplessness and resilience changed my life.

"When will we also teach them what they are?

We should say to each of them:
Do you know what you are?
You are a marvel. You are unique.
In all the years that have passed,
there has never been another child like you.
Your legs, your arms, your clever fingers,
the way you move.
You may become a Shakespeare,
a Michelangelo, a Beethoven.
You have the capacity for anything.
Yes, you are a marvel.
And when you grow up, can you then harm
another who is, like you, a marvel?
You must work; we must all work,
to make the world worthy of its children."

Pablo Casals

Why do Some Kids Thrive Under Pressure and Other Fall Apart?

"Resilience is the human capacity to face, overcome and be strengthened by or even transformed by the adversities of life. Everyone faces adversities; no one is exempt… With resilience, children can triumph over trauma; without it, trauma (adversity) triumphs. The crises children face both within their families and in their communities can overwhelm them."

A Guide to Promoting Resilience in Children: Strengthening the Human Spirit
The International Resilience Project and the Bernard Van Leer Foundation

How do we teach children to enjoy learning and really love school? How do we engage children in the learning process so that they do not drop out of school, in their minds in the early years and with their bodies in the later ones? How do we as parents and educators instill good self-esteem in our young people? What kind of world would we have if we raised our children to believe in themselves as learners and really like themselves?

The answer to these questions is actually quite simple: we teach our infants, toddlers, preschoolers, elementary and secondary school children to be resilient and have a growth mindset. We provide them with kid-friendly strategies for success, proven by decades of research, allowing them to take ownership in their own learning and feel pride in their accomplishments. Excitement about learning turns on the good neurotransmitters in the brain giving pride in learning. Challenging oneself through effort and problem solving after failure increases the neural networks in the brain and makes the children smarter.

Resilience is defined as a person's ability to snap back in response to adversity. It is the ability to keep on working on hard tasks and constructively deal with setbacks and problems. It is working to solve the situation instead of staying down for the count being thoroughly discouraged. It is the response of jumping back up to reassure yourself when faced with stress, threat or trauma.

Resilience can be boosted by direct training and practice, by emphasizing what children can say and do to stay focused on the goal and keep working after they take a hit or fail at a task. Dean Becker, who developed the resilience training program *Adaptive Learning Systems* said, "More than education, more than experience, more than training, a person's level of resilience will determine who succeeds and who fails."

Resilience is highly connected to one's self-identity and how the world is construed. Resilience is defining yourself as being a winner who succeeds because of strong inner values and effective coping skills. Victim beliefs decrease when children learn new skills and view themselves as being able to stay the course to get a job done. Social psychologist Albert Bandera said, "In order to succeed, people need a sense of self-efficacy, to struggle together with resilience to meet the inevitable obstacles and inequities of life."

Alain de Botton said, "A good half of the art of living is resilience." Certain personal abilities that help a person manage adverse events are tied to temperament and genetics; however, strategies to develop psychological well being can be taught to children from a very young age. They can be taught that they can change their outlook and regulate high emotional arousal so that they don't become a victim of the mass negativity prevalent in our culture. A low level of resilience is associated with poor self-control and giving up easily on challenging tasks. The good news is that we can teach children to become resilient. But how do we teach children to become strong and identify with being winners?

The Positive Psychology Movement

A positive revolution is underway in the field of psychology. The concept of teaching children to become resilient comes from the Positive Psychology research of Martin Seligman and his colleagues at the University of Pennsylvania's *Penn Resilience Program*. This field of research has made a huge impact on how we see ourselves as learners and adapt life strategies that help make us happy. Since the time of Freud, the field of psychology had focused on people's problems. Seligman and others are studying successful, happy people to determine what they do right.

Happiness is not about owning things or chasing experiences and addictions. The art of happiness comes down to having a good character and practicing virtue. Peterson and Seligman have identified six virtues and twenty four character strengths that happy people consistently reported the wide world over. They called these skills "Signature Strengths." Much of success in life is associated with keeping a positive state of mind and connecting with others in loving relationships. Seligman said, "The definition of a character strength is that it contributes to fulfillment, strengths of the heart— zest, gratitude, hope and love are more robustly associated with life satisfaction than are the more cerebral strengths such as curiosity and love of learning." Programs and activities that teach children to learn how to be happy have a notable effect on good mental health and deterring alcohol and drug use and crime.

Character is important because it is intimately tied to self-esteem—how you see yourself and subsequently the choices that are made! I suspect that some forms of depression are due to "slippage of character." Negative life events happen and negative beliefs build up around them centering on the idea that life is not fair and nothing you do makes a difference, so why try? Bad stuff happens. Without the tools for resilience, discouragement and giving up can come up big time. Turning to addictions (whether from boredom, for thrills or as a way to deal with stress) results in a decrease in self-esteem.

We can teach children about the true meaning of happiness. The happiness research is very clear about what values, behaviors and choices that create a happy life. It is important to get children thinking about the priorities they choose which in turn determine who they become. Martin Seligman described the three types of happiness: "Happiness' is a scientifically unwieldy notion, but there are three different forms of it you can pursue. For the 'Pleasant Life,' you aim to have as much positive emotion as possible and learn the skills to amplify positive emotion. For the 'Engaged Life,' you identify your highest strengths and talents and recraft your life to use them as much as you can in work, love, friendship, parenting, and leisure. For the 'Meaningful Life,' you use your highest strengths and talents to belong to and serve something you believe is larger than the self."

Stress Inoculation: Fail a Little and Learn from It

We feel stressed and become overwhelmed when we believe that we don't have the necessary skills and resources to deal with unhappy events. Feelings of helplessness and dread build up when we are faced with a situation that we don't think we can handle. It is the perception of not being able to cope or successfully navigate a tricky situation, not the event itself.

Seligman says that 30% of American children suffer from depression. Pessimistic children are at much higher risk for becoming depressed than optimistic children. The research from Positive Psychology shows that children can become "depression proofed" by learning the social skills required for doing well in life. They can be taught tools and techniques to reverse the epidemic of hopelessness and "I don't care" attitude that accompanies giving up and becoming a slacker in life.

Seligman's concepts of Learned Helplessness and Learned Optimism have given a greater understanding of the thinking patterns that lie under depression. Seligman said, "The optimists and the pessimists: I have been studying them for the past twenty-five years. The defining characteristic of pessimists is that they tend to believe bad events will last a long time, will undermine everything they do, and are their own fault. The optimists, who are confronted with the same hard knocks of this world, think about misfortune in the opposite way. They tend to believe defeat is just a temporary setback, that its causes are confined to this one case. The optimists believe defeat is not their fault: Circumstances, bad luck, or other people brought it about. Such people are unfazed by defeat. Confronted by a bad situation, they perceive it as a challenge and try harder. I have found, however, that pessimism is escapable. Pessimists can in fact learn to be optimists, and not through mindless devices like whistling a happy tune or mouthing platitudes but by learning a new set of cognitive skills."

Seligman suggested using the vaccine model of immunizing children against stress and depression by teaching learning to deal with failure in small bits and overcoming it through effort. Children should be taught how to deal with failure as it is part of learning. Trial and error learning, which is making a mistake, learning from it and trying again, teaches persistence and self-mastery and is a valid form of learning.

Stress inoculation is tackling hard things in small doses, allowing failure and finding that you can handle it. It is learning to deal with a small amount of stress so that when big events happen, the coping skills to deal with it have been learned. As the difficulty of the stressor increases, the child gradually learns to deal with it thereby becoming inoculated against failure. Choosing to try another way when frustrated instead of giving in builds a good character.

Seligman challenged the permissive self-esteem movement that promoted praising of children for non effort believing it was detrimental to a child's well being. The "everyone-gets-a-trophy" movement has created a generation of entitled children who do not value the ethics of hard work which creates true self-esteem. He emphasized that children develop a solid self-esteem through effort and experiencing mastery, persistence, overcoming frustration and boredom, and meeting challenges. These are the skills recognized and rewarded by the real world. Self-esteem is gained by doing well through action and hard work not through empty praise. With this approach, the child perceives him or herself as someone who can handle difficult tasks. In addition, Seligman stated that children should not be given a sugar-coated life but be allowed to feel their negative emotions and use them as signals that something needs changing.

Teach a Growth Mindset to Help Children Succeed in Life

"It seems like the dialogue that we develop inside of ourselves as we learn something new is key to staying with it. Are we our own worst bully as we try to learn, or do we develop the mental prowess to encourage ourselves and look for the moments of joy in what we do?"

Christopher Gumz

Children understand that things happen for a reason. Even toddlers begin to grasp cause and effect as they try to figure out the world. Children tell themselves about how they did on a task. What they say to themselves makes a difference whether they keep on working or not.

Carol Dweck is a Stanford University professor whose research has shaped our understanding of how children motivate themselves to keep working after they fail. In her early research, Dweck gave children of similar intelligence unsolvable math problems. She observed that when they failed, the children chose one of three patterns to attack the problems. Some gave up, some buckled down and tried harder and there was an in-between group. She called the group of children who kept trying Mastery Oriented. She then asked the children to talk out loud while they faced the failure tasks.

Dweck identified the self-statements that Mastery Oriented children made to keep themselves on task after failing. The child's internal talk or explanatory styles or how he or she explained the failure or success determined their mastery or failure in future tasks. The Mastery Oriented children said things like, "This is a challenge. I'll try it this way. I'll get it. The children who gave up made statements of "I'm no good at math. I hate this. It's too hard. I want to get out of here."

Dweck's later research explored how to optimize self-esteem in children by emphasizing having a growth or "Can Do, Will Do" mindset. In numerous studies, she and her colleagues found that it is not intelligence and talent that creates success in a life but whether a person has a growth or fixed mindset. A growth mindset is having the belief that you can change if you apply yourself to a task. It is the belief that people are not set in concrete and that they can change. People with growth mindsets understand that intelligence and personal abilities are not set in stone, but improve with effort. Growth mindsets foster effort, hard work and seeing difficult tasks as a challenge.

Children with fixed mindsets believe that their intelligence or ability in an area is stable and can't be improved. They become discouraged and give up when work seems hard and say, "I'm not good at this. It's too hard. I don't care about this stuff. It's boring. Why bother?" Growth mindset thinkers outperform fixed mindset students. Fixed mindset thinkers have trouble when math becomes progressively harder and tell themselves that they don't have an aptitude for it.

Fixed mindset youngsters have more difficulty transitioning into high school and college as the work gets more challenging and they don't have the inner confidence to push through self-doubt and frustration to learn new skills. Lower expectations of being able to learn leads to lower achievement and avoidance of the higher levels of math and science.

Research showed that high school students with fixed mindsets are more likely to have negative feelings of shame about themselves. They expressed more negative feelings of hatred towards others people they did not like. Students with a growth mindset had positive attitudes, helped others and were more forgiving. It makes sense, if you have good self-esteem and like yourself, you are more likely to be kind to others.

Studies showed that although ideas about prejudice and aggression were fixed in some student's minds, a six-week intervention that taught growth mindset decreased aggression and hostility and increased cross-racial interaction. The control group that only taught conflict skills to deal with social adversity did not change in their aggression rates. Students in both groups reported a reduction in depression when compared with the no-treatment group. Changing mindsets along with teaching skills to deal with social conflict and stress made the difference in helping students deal with social stressors and decreasing aggression.

Dweck and her colleagues are exploring other areas of the malleable character of human nature and how it relates to how people think of themselves and also about different groups with long-standing conflict such as Israel and Pakistan. The conclusion from many growth mindset studies is that we are people who can change *if we think we can*. "Whether you think you can or think you can't— you're right," said Henry Ford.

The research consistently shows that we need to teach children how to think and that their potential in an area of endeavor is not limited. Teach them that adversity is a part of life that they can deal with it as part of a life-learning process. Teach children how to think about their emotions, abilities, talents, needs, beliefs and goals and how their brain circuits can be changed by positive thinking. Teach them to cope with social adversity and to view different groups of people (bullies and victims and different cultures and races who are seen as belligerent) as not bad or evil but misguided and able to grow and change.

Process Praise: Applaud Effort not Intelligence, Looks or Talent

Dweck's research showed that parents and teachers who praise children for their personal (fixed) qualities such as intelligence, talent and ability may actually jeopardize a child's success. A child's belief that they are special because they are intelligent or beautiful is a trap that tells them that they don't have to work hard so that they will grow. Children who are praised for their talents rest on their laurels and become unproductive. They don't learn the skills for dealing with frustration when stuck on learning a new task. One study found that individuals with low self-esteem felt worse about themselves after repeating positive self-statements. Self-affirmations don't work unless they are accompanied by a growth mindset: thinking that hard work and becoming excited about learning from mistakes are the key to achieving the goal. It is not enough to keep repeating positive statements. Thomas Edison said, "I haven't failed. I've just found 10,000 ways that won't work."

American youngsters who have less responsibility seem to have more trouble maturing than teenagers in other countries. Our society's emphasis on immediate gratification, material objects, video games and technology, celebrity worship and an entertainment-oriented lifestyle gives rise to the idea that things are boring if they are not effortless and fun. Children with learning challenges who have learned to give up due to high frustration at not being able to learn a skill profit immensely from resilience training. Gifted children who have uneven talents and development may be at risk for giving up when they hit an area that is not easy for them and may suffer depression. People with natural talents can coast on their abilities without effort for only so long. However, if they harbor the mentality of "I'm smart so I don't have to apply myself" they will meet challenges in the future that they are not mentally prepared for. Wanting to be famous without applying the effort results in empty dreams that lead nowhere.

Seligman's and Dweck's research helps counteract the superficiality emphasis that our children are exposed to. Dweck said, "If parents want to give their children a gift, the best thing they can do is to teach their children to love challenges, be intrigued by mistakes, enjoy effort, and keep on learning." She recommends the use of feedback statements and questions to children to encourage them to analyze the problem, make the decision to learn from it, and work hard.

Teacher Cues from Carol Dweck that Reinforce Effort and Foster Growth Mindset

You are in charge of your mind. You can help it grow by using it in the right way.
Wow, that was a really good score. You must have worked really hard.
What did you learn today?
What mistake did you make that taught you something?
What did you try hard at today?
What can you learn from this?
What will you do the next time you are in this situation?

I visited a second grade class when the teacher had the children making sit-upons from oil cloth stuffed with old magazines and sewn with yarn. The children punched holes in the oil cloth and used scotch tape to make a needle for the yarn. The tape wasn't stiff enough and the children complained that they couldn't do it. I thought that the task was too difficult for little fingers but the teacher insisted they could do it. With some coaching for those who had the most trouble, every child finished the task. She kept saying, "You can do this. Things worth doing are things to keep working at. You'll feel proud when you are done. Tell yourself that you will finish." She taught "effort statements" and there were smiles all around. I was wrong about the task being too hard to finish. This plucky teacher taught an object lesson of how to be a winner in life—keep on trying and tell yourself that you can do it! Along with that she taught character and coping with disappointment and failure.

Little Brains are Plastic: The Phenomenon of Neuroplasticity

Dr. Dweck said, "Brains can be developed like a muscle." The growth mindset approach is supported by neuroscience, which demonstrates the plasticity of the brain when it takes on new challenges. Research shows that those who think they can learn from their mistakes have a different brain reaction to mistakes. EEG brainwaves were taken of children while they completed a hard problem and then given feedback about their errors. Children with growth mindsets turned on areas of their brains when receiving new information and then correcting errors. The images of their brain waves showed that they processed new information about their mistakes deeply.

The research on neuroplasticity and how the brain can change with practice shows that neural networks repair themselves and add capacity when they are exercised by learning new skills. Eric Kandel, M.D. was a recipient of the 2000 Nobel Prize in Physiology or Medicine for showing that the number of synaptic connections in a neural bundle can double with an hour of stimulation on a task. Brains can actually be rewired through repetition and practice of the new skill that is being learned.

The same is true of thoughts. Thoughts repeated enough can affect the structure of your brain. The dark side to neural plasticity is that repeating a negative thought over and over reinforces that corresponding pathway in the brain. Repeated thoughts add to the capacity of the synaptic connections that carry information through your brain. Dr. Kandel also found that the brain efficiently prunes what it does not need. Unused neural pathways atrophy within a short time when they are not used. This exciting research suggests that by teaching positive cognitive skills and strategies, the neural wiring of the brain can be enhanced. We can teach children not only how to think, but how to think about maximizing their brains. In doing so, we help them make the best of what brainpower they have and increase it.

Little minds and brains are pliable as infants, toddlers and children "grow" their brains through environmental enrichment. They learn by tuning into the adult language around them. How we view their learning ability affects their personalities and subsequently their will power. Sometimes we focus on the wrong thing to boost our own self-esteem. Parents want to believe that their own child is smarter than others as in "I feel good if I have produced a smart child." Mothers who did what is called process praise of "Look at how hard you are trying" and "Wow, look at you figuring this out on your own," had five-year-olds who showed more growth mindsets and independence. Children of mothers who said "you are a genius or brilliant" and focused on intelligence or physical traits of being handsome or beautiful did not do as well.

The earlier we teach children how to think in ways that depression-proof themselves the better. Seligman said, "Teaching children learned optimism before puberty, but late enough in childhood so that they are metacognitive (capable of thinking about thinking), is a fruitful strategy. When the immunized children use these skills to cope with the first rejections of puberty, they get better and better at using these skills. Our analysis shows that the change from pessimism to optimism is at least partly responsible for the prevention of depressive symptoms."

Relational Trauma Affects Children's Mental Health

"There are three possible outcomes in each situation—winner, loser or learner.
Feelings can be losing, winning or learning. I wish you learning from your feelings...
To be conscious of the feelings and the body is to be mindful of the heart."

Virginia Satir

We learn to act out, suppress or express our emotions in healthy ways in our earliest relationships. The psychological research shows that having a sense of security and attachment at an early age is a biological necessity for learning new skills such as affect regulation, coping with stressors and experiencing intimacy. Children from supportive parents gradually learn to deal with emotional discomfort after a stressor and learn to tolerate some distress. Emotional self-regulation is the ability to respond to a situation with socially acceptable reactions as well as inhibiting unacceptable behaviors. Children who are well-liked by their peers seem to learn this skill on their own.

Most traumatizing experiences come from other people; being harmed by another person to the extent that the person feels confused, helpless and hopeless is called relational trauma. Relational trauma interrupts the child's normal, developmental learning process and he cannot learn to regulate his emotions. The Adverse Childhood Experiences long-term research study found that traumatic life events are the biggest cause of anxiety, depression and other mental health problems. Children who had early exposure to family violence, alcohol and drugs, family dysfunction, physical, sexual and emotional abuse, neglect by parents or caregivers, peer violence and witnessing community violence took tremendous hits to their mental and physical health that lasted a life time.

About two-thirds of the adults in the study reported that they had suffered one or more types of adversity. Of that group, 87 percent said that they experience two or more types. These events did not happen in isolation. Certain adverse experiences created the climate where others happened. For example, an alcoholic, raging father who left the home opened the stage for other boyfriends of the mother moving in who might engage in verbal, physical or sexual abuse of the children. Having a single mother who struggled financially meant living in low-rent neighborhoods where there was more exposure to community violence, drugs and gangs. The more adverse categories of adverse childhood experienced increased their odds of having behavior and learning problems in school as many as thirty-two times as compared to children who didn't. They were unable to trust adults had difficulty with peer relationships and became chronic underachievers.

Children who lived with toxic stress and danger most of their lives experience the world as an out-of-control place. They are frequently in the fight, flight or freeze mode and their brains become overloaded with the stress hormones of cortisol and adrenalin. They used food, alcohol, cigarettes, drugs, inappropriate sex and high-risk activities as solutions to escape from their problems. As adults, they had a higher risk for obesity, medical and mental illness. They were more likely to have greater problems at work and to have spent time in prison.

Children raised in families with higher rates of violence are at greater risk for being physically aggressive toward their siblings and later on their own children or romantic partner. Parental physical punishment of the adolescent has been associated with later dating violence. Parents who do not monitor their children's behavior or give inconsistent discipline create children who do not have the social skills to succeed in happy relationships.

Children with critical, angry or perfectionist parents need these lessons on how to deal with emotional overload and failure more than children from more supportive families. Children need comforting and discussions about the daily issues they face so they can address and talk through their fears. Parents are not always available to talk to their children. One study showed that low-income mothers who had experienced their own childhood traumas had "traumatic avoidance symptoms" and were unable to address thoughts, emotions, sensations or memories of those traumas. This avoidance interfered with their ability to talk to their children about problems and emotions.

At-Risk Children and Emotional Dysregulation

Cuts to Medicaid, welfare, mental health services, child care subsidy and substance abuse programs and children and family services have pushed some families to the edge. Parents who were raised in dysfunctional home often use the same poor stress management techniques and harsh parenting practices that they were raised with. Research shows that even harsh parenting such as grabbing a child's arm, cursing and saying that they are no good releases stress hormone in children's brains. Ongoing negative feedback which causes a child to believe that he or she is worthless makes them feel helpless to impact their lives. The levels of the stress hormones of cortisol, alpha amylase, nerve growth factor and immunoglobulin is higher in children from families where there is poverty. In harsh and punishing environments where a child does not feel safe, there is damage to the amygdala, the child can become inattentive, hyperactive and has problems taking in and retaining new learning.

In addition to ongoing negativity, parental neglect is a major reason today for children being removed from their homes. Rejection hurts! Brain imaging studies have shown that physical pain and social rejection turned on the same areas of the brain. In my county in Arizona, sixty-seven percent of dependency cases where children were removed from their homes, drugs and alcohol were a contributing factor. As hard drugs become more cheap and accessible, more parents are unable to care for their children and more babies are born addicted. Having beliefs of things being beyond one's personal control creates feelings of stress. The confusion surrounding a child in foster care furthers the cycle of generational abuse and chaos. Feeling helpless and daily stress translates into long-term adverse effects on learning, memory and health outcomes across the lifetime.

Children from high-risk, low-income homes who faced early adversity have more problems in the transition to school, which gives them increased risk for early school failure and when they move on to higher learning. When there is chaos, abuse or neglect at home, the child is deprived of soothing support and the necessary stimulation to produce brain growth. Normal childhood development is disrupted, leaving the child empty and needy and fearful of being rejected and abandoned. The stressors that poverty brings can lead to health problems and diseases throughout their lives, causing some to die at an early age. Children from conflictual homes become easily stressed as their world is not predictable and trauma memories became deep-wired in their nervous systems.

Researchers have identified changes in the brains of children who have grown up in poverty that can lead to lifelong problems like depression, learning difficulties and limitations in the ability to cope with stress. One study linked later learning problems to poor processing of auditory information. However; the extent of those negative brain changes was influenced strongly by whether a parent was *attentive and nurturing*. In the absence of a loving parent, relatives, teachers and outside people who gave the child encouragement and social support helped mitigate some of the effects of a chaotic home. A loving, enriched environment reduces anxiety and helps children shift out of bad moods so they can focus on learning. Research shows that anxiety can be decreased by making nurturing changes to their environment through positive adults who showered attention and love on children.

Parents whose lives are constantly in emotionally and financial upheaval often don't have good coping mechanisms to deal with stress. Children from neglectful or chaotic homes often are unable to regulate strong emotions. They can't develop the necessary internal resources to learn how to calm themselves as they don't have time to recover from one aversive event to another. Instead they turn to more primitive, tension-reducing strategies of suppression of feelings through addictive activities, distraction or anger outbreaks. They become overly responsive to small stressors and feel hurt and rejected easily or feel threatened and react with hostility.

Dr. Gail Wagnild, the creator of *The Resilience Scale*™, noted that the more resilient children showed a pattern of low emotional and hormonal arousal with lowered heart rates and skin conductance, and a higher intensity of stimuli are needed to stimulate them. At-risk children who had stronger self-regulation in kindergarten scored 15 points higher on a math test in first grade, 11 points higher on a reading test, and nearly seven points higher on a vocabulary test than at-risk children with weaker self-regulation.

Temperament and Coping with Life's Stressors

The temperament studies demonstrate that some infants and children respond to stress with a higher level of physiological arousal and distress. Children from the same family can differ in their emotional reactions with some having a more robust central nervous system that helps them become more resilient. Although raised in the same home, they have a different set of genes that are hyper-responsive to stimuli. Their central nervous systems and hormonal reactions handle change or stressors more efficiently. They become easily aroused due to the over-reactivity of their brain and central nervous system and register more events as harmful.

As infants, they experience high-arousal, have muscle tension, faster heart rates and elevated cortisol responses to stress and develop affect regulation difficulties and become anxious. They grow up to have more difficulty with changes in their life. They are more likely to distort the amount of harm they perceive due to their over-stimulated central nervous system which reacts to the stress hormones. They become overly selective to their own internal negative arousal and interpret things through their own exaggerated emotional response. They distort ideas of danger based on their heightened physiological arousal. Brain studies showing this type of arousal pattern portray an overly-reactive amygdala.

Other children are harder to soothe from birth and exhibit more agitation and unhappiness. They become the temperamentally difficult and strong-willed children who are harder to teach and discipline. They are more high-strung and easily frustrated and implosive. Some are more aggressive and irritable and have a temperament that responds quickly to frustration. High-demand children are hyper-focused in going after what they want and are masters at avoiding outside distractions. They dig in to and badger adults to attain their goal and become angry when thwarted. They have short-lived pleasure in obtaining their materialistic goals. They have a higher-than-average interest in novelty and seek highly-pleasurable activities placing them at earlier risk for alcohol and drugs. Children with irritable temperaments and entitled personalities don't have the ability to tune in to their emotions and process them.

Common Coping Patterns of Children from Dysfunctional Families

Developing Anger

Anger can be a reaction to feeling threatened or helpless and results in a coping style of needing to be in control. The energy of self-indulgent anger in parents is contagious just like a cold that infects a family. Each family member is affected by the anger in their social system and acts it out in their own unique way whether cowering in silence with resentment or turning their anger on others. The universal desire to survive during situations of threat is linked with high physiological arousal and anger. The hormones, increased muscle tension, and pounding heart are all activated as an automatic response and a protective mechanism which "revs" up the body to deal with threat. Prolonged, excessive chaos in the child's home leads to brain and hormonal changes resulting in withdrawal due to fear and acting out. Anxiety, frustration and agitation flavor how they view life.

Studies show that people experience a diminished sense of control when stressed and they become anxious. The inability to tolerate or deal with anxious feelings when stressed can exaggerate the need to control someone or something. Anger is an energizing emotion that breaks into the anxiety as the person uses one feeling to alter another. Anger can be used as a substitute emotion to block anxiety that comes up from attempts to gain a sense of order and control over others. Often there is an unconscious entitlement belief of "I can get angry to stay in charge." The force of anger gets the other person to comply so it's a two-fold payoff: (1.) the feeling of being in control, and (2.) a reduction in inner anxiety.

Aggressive Behavior

Aggressive behavior can be learned from parents or siblings who get their way through hostility or violence. Children with a less-sensitive nature and a tougher outlook observe that there is a payoff for becoming angry when feeling stressed or threatened. They learn that the meanest, angriest dog gets the bone! They don't want to become a victim so act like the angry parent who ends up with the goodies;

this is called identification with the aggressor. These children identify with the dominant parent's manipulation and intimidation to get what is wanted. Dominance aggression in the family is carried on as the older children bully younger, weaker ones.

Feeling contemptuous for those who are weaker becomes a rationale for aggressive behavior by saying the weaker person deserved it. Aggressive children learn to suppress unwanted vulnerable emotions of shame and humiliation. They develop an inner arousal pattern where negative feelings are immediately shut down and anger is substituted. Anger becomes the immediate emotion when stressed or threatened. Children in families where feelings are treated with disrespect learn this defense and choose friends whose feelings they can attempt to control.

Being aggressive and cruel has a neurochemical basis. A brain-imaging study showed that bullies enjoyed seeing victims in pain. Activity in the pleasure systems of aggressive teenage boy's brains increased when they watched a video of someone being hurt. In another study, the brain scans of dominant, aggressive monkeys showed increased brain flow activation in the pleasure center which releases dopamine when they terrorized low-status monkeys.

These studies show the underpinnings of sadistic behavior—that bullies get a brain buzz when they are aggressive. This is a learned association between inflicting emotional or physical pain and the discharge of the feel-good chemicals of the brain. Bullying can lead to dopamine overdrive. One study showed that children who bully are more likely to act aggressively again if they witness their victim's submissiveness. This neurotransmitter aspect to bullying behavior, which has not yet been addressed fully by the psychological research, is explored in my Flash interactive video for children called *Bullying - It's Not Okay to Feel Good by Making Others Feel Bad* at www.angriesout.com or on YouTube at http://www.youtube.com/watch?v=DAI9k9bhHIc.

Rebelling against Authority

Some children who come from stable homes rebel against the positive values in their families; this pattern seems to be related to a temperament style of taking high risks to increase dopamine in the brain. Other families are rebellious against the rules that make society run smoothly and do not correct their children for bullying or fighting. Some families engage in illegal actions for a livelihood and have pride in flaunting rules. They give their children permission to break the rules of society that help others live in safety. They foster an entitlement belief in their children of "I am special and I get to do what I want," "Rules don't apply to me," and "Don't mess with me." Rebellion and defiance can also take the form of refusing reasonable requests because of a dislike of authority and being told what to do.

Dissociation: Becoming Anxious, Numb and Spacing Out

Freezing is the common reaction to threat and confrontation of the "fight, flight or freeze" coping strategies harkening back to our cave man history. Dissociation is a typical human response to deal with threat as a way of staying safe in situations of threat. Becoming confused, overwhelmed, "losing one's tongue" and going into shock are all forms of dissociation. When the child cannot engage in fighting or running away, he becomes overwhelmed and runs away in his mind. Numbing and freezing the body allows the person to avoid being flooded with intense emotions. Shame and hurt accompany this response and the person feels robbed of his power.

Dissociating prevents the person from dealing with the real world as he has "checked out" of his normal ability to function. It is said to be a survival response that helps a person deal with an overwhelming situation when he or she has no other options. Colin Ross, a past President of the International Society for the Study of Trauma and Dissociation, said that if we humans did not have the dissociative response, we would all be psychotic.

Becoming Hypervigilant

Anger and abuse in the home are disruptive to children. One way of coping for children is to become hyper alert in response to loud voices and anger as a means of survival and feeling safer. Hypervigilance is one of the symptoms of posttraumatic stress disorder. Children develop hyper alertness when they are overwhelmed by events they can't control. With hyperarousal, the automatic nervous system and parts of the brain become dysregulated with agitation, anxiety and feeling fragmented when experiencing the world as an unsafe place. Teaching children to breathe deeply when upset helps calm the agitated mind by adding oxygen to the body.

Developing a Fixed Mindset

Children who grow up in homes where parents make helpless victim statements learn this style of coping with adverse advents. Children of mothers who were discouraged by constant setbacks adopted the pessimistic "Why try? Nothing I do makes a difference" style of thinking. Seligman called this Learned Helplessness. Giving up when faced with stressors due to overwhelming feelings of helplessness helps keep generations of families mired in poverty.

Perfectionism, Fear of Failure and Avoiding Risks

Some children believe that they must be perfect in whatever they do. This backfires as they procrastinate about starting hard tasks and they avoid taking risks. Overachieving parents can give messages of needing to be perfect. Their children become overwhelmed with stress, self-criticism, anxiety and depression. Hovering parents with unrealistic expectations put too much pressure on a child for academic achievement. Children can live up or down to the expectations we choose for them. Expectations for young people should be high enough to challenge them to put forth a good effort but not so high that it overwhelms them.

Poor Self-regulation Skills

A recent survey from the Centers for Disease Control and Prevention stated that about 11 percent of children have been diagnosed with attention deficit hyperactivity disorder. Taking children from ages four to seventeen, this translates to nearly six and a half million children. Children from low-income homes with behavior and academic problems are likely to struggle with the learning demands of the classroom which require paying attention, auditory processing and impulse control.

A long-term research study focused on three to five year olds from low-income homes who attended Head Start. The self-regulation skills of being able to focus attention and inhibit impulsive responding were shown to be more important than intelligence for succeeding in academic subjects. Kindergarteners at risk for violence due to family and neighborhood influences were taught how to manage their impulsivity and negotiate conflict while their parents were taught anger management and how to model self-control. Follow up on the intervention ten years later showed a 48 percent reduction in arrests for murder and rape and a 52 percent reduction in the prevalence of conduct disorders. Another study showed that at-risk children who were taught these skills could more easily self-regulate their emotions and behavior, and attain higher reading, math and vocabulary achievement.

Affect regulation is the ability to recognize and calm one's emotions. Self-regulation is an important skill for developing and continuing friendships with others. Children who learn self-soothing to calm themselves when they are upset have higher self-esteem and less of a need later on to turn to alcohol and substances or act out their frustrations on other people.

It is important to learn how to calm one's self when triggered or upset and make a conscious decision to use self-instruction to quiet the emotions. Too often people act out to get away from the intense, internal arousal and to alleviate stress. Children and adults cope with stress and reduce tension by engaging in excessive behaviors that have an addictive-like quality. Some unhealthy coping strategies to deal with stress include eating too much, watching too much television, spending hours texting or playing video games, yelling and cursing, blaming others or insisting that someone else makes us feel better. Other dysfunctional behaviors such as cutting wrists, chewing fingernails, getting headaches or stomach aches, turn conflict into body symptoms. Other children withdraw emotionally or run away and hide.

Having Trust and Intimacy Disrupted

Many children suffer from early relational trauma that causes lack of trust in others. One estimate is that eighty percent of traumatized children are traumatized by their parents. Children from angry homes often are on guard and perceive some benign social situations as personally threatening. They have a hostile chip on their shoulders and split their world into good guys and bad guys, viewing the world through a lens of suspicion that others are out to harm them. They are unable to tolerate ambiguity in others and don't understand that others can have healthy and unhealthy traits concurrently without wishing them harm. They must remain diligent, keeping a constant lookout for harm. In doing so, they misread the environment and see danger when there is none.

Children who experience severe parental fighting, addictions, abuse or neglect have a hard time learning the positive social skills necessary for good relationships. They have what Michael Odent M.D. calls "an impairment to love." They observe that people hurt each other with words and actions. Fears of being safe and fears of intimacy as well as anger develop as their world is not safe. Later in life, they fear being engulfed and smothered by their partners so keep their distance emotionally. Withdrawal from emotional intimacy either quietly or with anger becomes a way to head off Richter-Scale anxiety.

Resilience Research Projects

Karen Reivich and Jane Gillham used Martin Seligman's concepts in their Penn Resiliency Program to provide resilience skill training for parents and teachers. They taught adults to model the skills of positive self-talk to elementary and middle school children. The program taught the skills of assertiveness, negotiation, decision-making and coping with difficult situations and emotions and social problem-solving and relaxation. They found that building resilience in younger children helped thwart depression. Gillham said, "Negative self-talk can create self-fulfilling prophecies, leading kids to behave in ways that create new situations that only reinforce the negative thoughts they have about themselves. Say, for example, that a child does poorly on an algebra test. That may prompt her to think, "I can't do math," fueling feelings of discouragement and sadness. Because of those thoughts, she stops studying and then bombs the next exam. A downward spiral ensues."

A Guide to Promoting Resilience in Children: Strengthening the Human Spirit was an international study that surveyed 589 children and their families and caregivers from different countries and cultures across the world. Primary author, Edith H. Grotberg, Ph.D. *of* The International Resilience Project and the Bernard Van Leer Foundation developed the *Early Childhood Development: Practice and Reflections* series. The authors concluded that cultures vary in how the adults teach their young people about resilience and dealing with adversity. The authors stated that, "Some cultures rely more on faith than on problem solving in facing adversity. Some cultures are more concerned with punishment and guilt while others discipline and reconcile. Some cultures expect children to be more dependent on others for help in adversity rather than becoming autonomous and more self-reliant. The parents in some countries maintain a close relationship with their children while others 'cut off' their children at about age five. The resilient children manage this kind of rejection; non-resilient children withdraw, submit and are depressed." The research concluded that no matter whether the adults were supportive or neglectful, resilient children were better prepared to have a successful future.

Some families have that old sturdy, pioneer spirit as they face hardships. They model getting through adversity and staying strong to their children. Here are some resilience statements heard in my private psychology practice during the recession when families were facing home foreclosure:

- "I will land on my feet just like a cat. And if I don't, I'll roll over and spring back up."

- "There is another side to this. The side I choose to be on is called survival."

- "We are family. We will stick together through this and make it through."

- "We may be down at the moment, but we are not out. Don't count us out."

- "If things are not working, stop where you are, turn and go another direction. There are many directions, many paths, and many roads that you haven't gone down yet."

Resilience Strategies that Well-functioning People Use after

Experiencing Stress and Trauma

Accepting that challenges and setbacks are part of life.

Incorporating stress management techniques to tame unhealthy stress responses.

Reinterpreting negative events to give them different meanings (cognitive reappraisal).

Hanging tough by giving self-reassurance that stressful events and hard times can be dealt with.

Viewing adversity as life lessons to be dealt with giving opportunity for self-growth and wisdom.

Interrupting victim beliefs and defeatist attitudes.

Changing pessimistic thinking and a negative outlook on life.

Enhancing positive emotions and avoiding depression through self-talk and positive strategies.

Facing fears rather than avoiding or running from them.

Observing rather than overreacting to adverse situations.

Decreasing catastrophizing (What if this bad thing happens?).

Imitating resilient role models in real life, fiction and biographies.

Keeping a strong social network--Reaching out and maintaining positive friends and mentors.

Avoiding the Drive-Through Mood Disorder—Excessive fast food meant poor nutrition which affects the mood.

Developing a strong body—self-esteem is enhanced when the body is physically fit.

Developing family connections, memories and sayings that promote a sense of unity and strength.

Teaching Social Skills through Cues Given by Parents and Teachers

Children enjoy learning about social skills that will ease their way in the world. Cues from adults are a valid way of instruction for teaching social skills. Positive cues give the child who misbehaves an immediate alternative regarding what he can do. Overly-emotional children can be taught how to self-regulate their emotions by learning self-soothing. Children with distractibility can be taught to persist on a task when they become frustrated or angry. The use of your correctly-phrased cue after disruptive or unwelcome behavior is one of the most important tools that you have in your arsenal of teaching techniques.

To succeed in school as well as in life children need self-regulation skills, which is called "executive functioning." This includes planning and organizing work, controlling their effort, paying attention and staying on task. Not having these skills creates adjustment problems and impedes learning as the child does not focus and stay on task. In essence some children need to learn skills on how to learn.

Social cues such as eye contact, smiling, listening, asking appropriate questions, etc. are important in making and maintaining friendships. Children with learning disabilities and those who are socially awkward do not naturally pick up on cues to ease social situations. They require direct teaching and teacher cues of how to react to conflict and feelings of being overwhelmed. You can help clueless children develop some sort of social antenna of how their actions have consequences.

When parents and teachers comfort an upset child and help him or her solve the problem that had caused the emotional outburst, the child learns to work through uncomfortable feelings with less shame. Boys require extra cueing as they are typically socialized to hide or discount their negative emotions. Aggressive children who repress their emotions need extra emotional support and skill teaching from caring adults. Positive teacher cues do not belittle or shame the child but help him or her save face by instructing him what he can do to take care of himself. They remind him to make a responsible choice to act in ways that help him feel good. Your repeating a cue that gives instruction and hope helps the child internalize the message as his own.

Tell the child that you believe in his or her ability to figure out his problem plus give information as to how he might take care of himself. A positive message about how to act appropriately can be an effective and humane thing you can do for a child who is hurting. The message comes through again and again—you believe in and support his or her autonomy and ability to work things out for his best interests. This brings about the self-fulfilling prophecy of "Someone believes in me so I must have what it takes to work out the threatening situation!"

New skills require effort and motivation to get past discomfort and self-doubt. Practice, practice, practice is needed before a new skill becomes automatic. "Any sequence of mental action which has been frequently repeated tends to perpetuate itself," said William James. Regular practice simply isn't enough. Top achievers do deliberate practice. They develop strategies to stay focused and goal oriented and allow feedback on their performance. They know that to be really good at something they have to actually practice failing and then learn from their mistakes. The concentrated focus pays off. After a while they go on auto pilot where they have achieved a new comfort zone with that task to get to that "OK Plateau" where there is smooth sailing.

Repetition is the best way to learn a new skill. Learning these cues takes minimal effort on your part and will give you a thousand-fold return on your investment of time. Use Post It Notes to yourself on your desk as a reminder to use teacher cues. Add new cues to your teaching repertoire gradually by practicing one cue for several days until you hear yourself saying it automatically in response to children's fixed mindset statements. Share these cues with the parents of the children so that they can use them at home also.

Teaching children how to think for themselves and become autonomous from adult intervention when faced with a learning or social stressor gives them tools for life. Here are some teacher cues I overheard from a brilliant teacher who encouraged problem-solving skills in three-year-old children who had language delays and severe behavior problems:

- Come up with a strategy of how you are going to break into negative thoughts.
- You can figure this out. Go talk to _____ and get a plan. Then come back and run it by me.
- You are smart enough to know how to handle this without getting upset.
- I wonder what positive things you will say to yourself when things get tough?
- Put your heads together and come up with something different than fighting.
- Tell him you don't like what he is doing. Tell him to stop. Stick up for yourself.

Intrinsic Learning: Cognitive Reappraisals, Cognitive Control and Helper Words

Cognitions are the thoughts, beliefs and ideas that we typically use. We give meanings to what happens to us and define ourselves and ultimately our destiny by what we say and think. As the early Stoics and psychologists William James and Albert Ellis have taught, our emotions and behaviors come from the meanings we give to what happened. It is not what happens to us per se, but how we think about it and what we do. We humans have the ability to use awareness and insight to change our thinking.

Love of learning starts with our inner language and intrinsic reinforcement—the positive things that we say to ourselves to make us masters of our own fate. The philosopher Horace said, "Rule your mind or it will rule you." Identity and self-esteem are dependent on how we language ourselves whether it is in speaking out loud or with our inner, private speech.

Self-talk phrases that empower people are from the Cognitive Behavioral psychology approach. Behavioral self-control can come from self-instruction of words or phrases to interrupt negative, self-defeating thoughts to change one's attitude, feelings and actions. Children can learn to verbalize directions, ask themselves questions, give instructions and reinforce themselves to interrupt inappropriate actions and impulsivity, problem solve, stay on task, assess their progress and change how they see a problem.

Cognitive Reappraisal and Post Traumatic Growth

"When a man is pushed, tormented, defeated, he has a chance to learn something."

Ralph Waldo Emerson

The psychological strategy of cognitive reappraisal is examining a problematic situation to gain a new perspective. Research shows that some people come through horrific events rather well if they take a philosophical attitude to what happened to them—sort of a survive and thrive mentality that is at the heart of a new movement in psychology called Posttraumatic Growth (PTG) which views adversity as a springboard for growth.

Posttraumatic stress disorder (PTSD) is a severe psychological reaction to an event that is outside the range of normal human experience. An estimated 7.8% of people are affected by events that stress them so that they remain affected sometimes across their lifetime. Specific trauma events such as child abuse, vehicle accidents, war tragedies, rape, natural disasters and other horrific events can create PTSD. Ongoing chronic stress and emotional pain such as prolonged parental fighting, being bullied and general family chaos can create an ongoing over reactive emotional condition. Often the person's innocence and beliefs that the world is safe change after a traumatic insult to the person where he or she feels helpless and hopeless. Other common symptoms of PTSD include flashbacks of memories, nightmares, intrusive thoughts, confusion, memory dissociation, exaggerated startle response, hyperarousal and loss of hope.

But wait, there is hope! Researchers Richard Tedeschi and Lawrence Calhoun and others from around the globe are proving that trauma can be an impetus for facilitating purpose and meaning in life and creating a growth-orientated mindset to increase resiliency. Specific Posttraumatic Growth changes include increased self-discipline, achieving a greater understanding of others, gaining a broader perspective on life, choosing better priorities and finding meaning in life.

Posttraumatic Growth is defined as those uplifting psychological changes that happen after dealing with and processing highly challenging life trauma events. Most often, PTSD and the growth process happen along side of each other. PTG includes those changes in a person's personality after struggling with trying to understand and come to grips with what happened to them. Posttraumatic growth responses are adaptive and life affirming as the person decides to move ahead and make something of their life. Tedeschi and Calhoun created *The Posttraumatic Growth Inventory* which helps us understand how people reappraise their lives using these dimensions and values.

Appreciation of life.
    Priorities about what is important in life.
    Appreciation for the value of one's life.
    Appreciating each day.

Increased ability to relate to and count on others.
    Feeling a sense of closeness with others.

Putting effort into relationships.
Learning how wonderful people can be.
Acceptance of needing others.

Openness to new possibilities.
Establishing a new path for life.
Ability to do better things with life.
Staying open to new opportunities.
Changing things that need changing.

Increased personal strength.
Feelings of self-reliance.
Acceptance of how things worked out.
Discovering you are stronger than you thought you were.

Positive spiritual change.
Gaining a deeper understanding of spiritual matters.
Developing a stronger religious faith.

Growth strategies such as cognitive reappraisals of viewing a challenging situation assist with Posttraumatic Growth cognitive reappraisals alter emotional responses by changing the interpretation of what the difficult situation means from being seen as impossible to doable. Putting a new picture frame or reframing around an old issue can lessen its negative emotional impact. Seeing a bad situation in a different light decreases the negative stress response. Identifying and challenging irrational thinking helps influence one's mood by counteracting over reactive beliefs to calmer ones.

Helper Words also are reappraisals of a negative situation where the child learns positive word to say to him or herself to change his perceptions of his ability to keep working. Sensitive internalized messages can remind a child to choose appropriate behavior and that he or she is in control of their inner state and more in charge of the situation.

Reduced cognitive control narrows a person's perception and he or she falls back to the primitive coping responses. Teaching self-instruction helps children gain a sense of responsibility which leads to a sense of control in one's life and increases confidence and optimism. Self-talk is featured in the children's books, *The Little Engine That Could*, who says, "I think I can," and *Bob the Builder* who asks, "Can we fix it?" Intrinsic motivation is having an internal standard for excellence, the motivation to do well and becoming caught in the momentum of the task.

Self-talk helps children draw on their internal or intrinsic motivation while completing a task so that will power does not become depleted. The completion of a challenging goal is a wonderful feeling that fosters future success. Teaching a child to self-monitor and carefully use his or her own reinforcement statements for hard work thus internalizes the love of learning and not being dependent upon outside reinforcement. Instead of your praising your children, teach them to praise themselves. Remind them to pat themselves only when they have worked hard and accomplished something. Internal reinforcement which a child will always have with him or her is much more powerful that an external reward.

What we want to do as parents and teachers is build an association between getting past frustration and moving forward on a new skill or hard task and feeling good inside. Associative learning happens when you build an association between working hard on a task and feeling good at the same time. The introduction of good feelings into a stressful situation overtakes the discouraged attitude thus keeping the child on task. The child develops an identity of being an excited learner. In addition teaching children cognitive control will enhance their ability to resist temptations and risky behaviors during their teenage years.

We can build a language of resilience in children through direct teaching of ideas that foster independence and problem solving. Direct teaching is an efficient way to impart instruction to children. You use direct teaching every day when you give reading and math instruction to groups of children. The same teaching principles apply to learning to be motivated. The small amount of time that you spend in rehearsing the children in positive self-talk statements will save you from time spent on teacher reprimands. Children can learn to promote a positive mindset in themselves and others. Children as young as three years of age can learn that making a mind adjustment makes them feel better.

Self-talk determines whether you persevere or not. As the Zen proverb says, "Be the master of your mind rather than mastered by your mind." Perseverance is a teachable skill that is learned from watching others successfully deal with their frustration when completing a hard task. Dear Abby said, "Perseverance is a skill that can be learned. Each time you succeed, you reinforce the idea that you can do it. The more that you do it, the better you will feel about yourself and it will be reflected in your work and social relationships." One of the biggest impacts you can have on a child's character is to teach them how to keep working when things are hard.

Research has found that between ages four and seven, children understand that people's thoughts and beliefs can both cause and reduce fear. Children can be taught to perceive and create a positive reality for their own success and happiness. Practice makes permanent. The outstanding UCLA basketball Coach John Wooden described this process in sports, "You have to apply yourself each day to becoming a little better. By applying yourself to the task of becoming a little better each and every day over a period of time, you will become a *lot* better."

Helper Words, as used here in this book, are positive phrases that children learn to say themselves to change their thinking and behavior. Teaching concepts of self-talk helps children develop an awareness of how much their internal talk determines their mood and subsequent behavior. As children who are prone to failure learn to change their thinking and focus on persistence, their learning tasks become easier.

Trial and Error Learning and Error Correction

Failure proof your children by teaching Error Correction. Errors in thinking are faulty thought patterns learned early in life that can lead to poor judgments, irrational demands, depression and not succeeding if life. Successful people make mistakes but face failure head on. One of the greatest ways to become successful is becoming comfortable with making a mistake and learning from it. Successive approximations or trial and error learning to get a task down pat is a valid form of learning. That is the basis of programmed reading and math workbooks.

Mistakes done well offer Teachable Moments! You can learn not only from your own mistakes but also from the failure of others. Chris DiBona, one of the managers at Google, said a wise statement that you could use in your classroom "I fail a lot, so I can help you with that." Your use of such statements that normalize making mistakes as part of the learning process helps children stop judging themselves and giving up after making a mistake.

Give the message that mistakes are a necessary option while learning something new. Your getting excited about making a mistake and learning from it is a skill that you can model for your children. Talk yourself out loud through a tough learning task so that your children overhear you. Say things like, "What am I missing here?" "What assumption have I made that is wrong?" "I'm getting frustrated, I'd better slow down and breathe," will help your children understand the process of getting through a difficult learning challenge.

Some Children Look Outside their Dysfunctional Families to Learn Different Values

Sometimes there are children from dysfunctional families who are wiser than their parents and know from an early age that things are not right in the family. This child understands he or she is different from the family in values and starts searching for a better way to live than to be mired in poverty or keep wounding each other with offensive behavior. He or she starts to look outside the home for positive role models—a teacher, neighbor, healthy relative, friend's parent or coach. If the child has talent, he is reinforced with attention and encouragement for his hard work. He becomes resilient in dealing with the dysfunction of the family and takes on the values of the outside world. His new identity becomes associated with achievement, hard work and increasing his talent for academics or sports.

Achievement and attainment of success becomes a survival strategy and a positive defense to bolster up self-esteem. The resilient child often becomes successful in life due to incorporation of strong work ethics. But a single focus can make the person a one-sided workaholic; a truly successful life requires all the skills necessary to form connections, a happy family and meaning in life. Later in life, the resilient child might choose to address those childhood traumas and dysfunctional family patterns that have taught him poor coping defenses.

We all have the need for social support and to belong. Most children who are not supported by the adults at home are hungry for adults in their lives who believe in them. Children need lifelines-- someone to reach out to. A supportive relationship with a positive adult outside the family helps children from dysfunctional homes cope more effectively. At-risk children who became successful in later life found someone to believe in them and encourage them. They formed alliances with teachers, counselors, coaches or other meaningful adults and adopted more healthy ways of coping with stress.

Resilient children from unhappy homes can learn values to become high achievers if they are supported by someone who encourages them to do their best. "I never talked to a successful adult who escaped from the underclass who didn't say there was some caring role model person in his or her life. We never know how important we may be to someone." said Virginia Cappeller, retired social worker and professor. We need other human beings to develop and grow.

For some young people, school may be the only haven they have. One teenager admitted, "The only positive adult attention I got was in school from some of the teachers. I knew which teachers liked me and I learned more from them. At home there weren't any adults who were interested in me so school became my favorite place to be."

Teachers and counselors are in a valuable position to become a meaningful force in young people's lives. You can be that life line for a child who may need that extra adult attention in his or her life. It might make all the difference in the world to a confused child who is trying to sort out his or her identity. Help them understand that after coming through a difficult time, they are in a good position to guide others who are facing similar challenges.

A child who does not have effective social support will lack the necessary experiences to fully develop certain centers of the brain. One major task in growing up and becoming a successful adult is to develop a sense of self and identity. Identity is defined by being in relationships. Identity is knowing and living who you are, and what you stand for. Introducing a child to the positive aspects of their surrounding adult world increases their awareness for better choices as they move through the adolescent years. A shared sense of identity in the family and in the larger community helps build that sense of belonging that fosters resilience.

Children become more secure in themselves when they know that they are valued and fit into the larger whole of the community and culture. Look up organizations in your area that offer children support and family activities. You might take a field trip or point out these opportunities to children. Being part of a church group, Scouts and Boys and Girls Clubs help children create a sense of belonging. Studies show that African American people who identify more strongly with their positive racial identity are generally happier as they identify with a strong family culture. Google *Information and Referral Helpline* and the name of your town for information on agencies for assistance for children.

Strategies to Teach Resilience to Children

Children have multiple self-esteems based on their competence in different areas. I tested a fourteen-year-old boy with learning disabilities and found him to be discouraged and depressed. Later that day walking past the pool hall in my town, I saw him confident and beaming as he was given some money that he had won. Although how he felt about himself as a learner was low, his self-esteem as a pool hustler was being developed. Chances are he will stay in the settings which stoke his self-esteem and it won't be the school/work world. Children define themselves as winners or losers with their different skill sets in different environments.

There are many areas where a child might develop a fixed mindset thus depriving himself of trying, advancing and mastering that skill. Think of specific children who are under your charge. In what areas does a child believe that his ability is fixed: intelligence, will power, math, sports, creative writing, playing a musical instrument, making friends and inhibiting impulsivity and aggression? Yes, there are natural talents where children excel. But to be well-rounded individuals who will succeed in our complex society, they should be given the mind tools that make them risk takers in trying new, beneficial activities.

We all have tasks and projects that we avoid because we aren't good at them. What areas do you believe that you are not good at and so you gave up before giving it a good effort? For me, it was statistics, and yes the other students had better abstract skills, but when I finally understood that it was my give-up attitude that caused me to fail, I buckled down and put forth immense effort to pass the course.

There are many well-researched coping skills associated with resilience and life-long satisfaction. This book of lesson plans features skills that give children positive social interactions, peer group acceptance, positive self-regard, and competency as learners and dealing with adversity. It teaches them to change their thinking about achievement, will power, motivation, failure and respecting themselves and others. Included here, in this book, are ideas and activities to assist children learning from these areas drawn from the psychological research:

- Social Skills
- Emotional Regulation
- Resilience and Effort Skills
- Stress Reduction
- Cognitive Restructuring
- Self Talk
- Behavioral Self-control
- Happiness Choices
- Signature Strengths and Character Skills

The positive psychological principles that create a happy life can be taught. I spent years in preschool and elementary classrooms and in a psychiatric hospital teaching groups of children the skills for emotional, social and vocational growth. The basic model I used to introduce a psychological new concept was

1. Identify the skill that is needed for the group at that specific age.
2. Develop a teaching dialogue about the concept with the age-appropriate language.
3. Facilitate a discussion about the concept using examples from the children's lives.
4. Read a book, watch a video, develop a play activity or create an art project to make the psychological concept specific and practical.
5. Ask open-ended questions and provide reinforcement for effort statements.
6. Use process praise where the child is reinforced for hard work and effort.

Praising for Effort

Hey, I've noticed how hard you've been studying and your grades show it.

Yes, that was a long, hard assignment but you stuck through it and mastered it.

Congrats, your time spent studying for your test really paid off in your grade.

You really worked hard and learned some tough material. Impressive!

You kept trying new strategies until you figured out what worked. That's called persistence.

The hours of effort you put in earned you that good grade. That really worked!

I noticed how you stayed with your homework and put great concentration on it.

Yes this project is going to take a lot of work, but I believe in your getting through it.

You are the kind of kid who gets things done.

Whew! You did it. It was a tough job but you stuck to it and got it done.

You stayed at your desk and kept your focus until the job was done. That's great!

This year we are going to learn some difficult material. I'm here for you.

You're going to learn a lot of great things because you know how to get the job done.

You are one hard worker, you know that? You should feel proud of yourself.

For students who breeze right through things, throw them a challenge. "Well you got through that in a hurry so it must be too easy for you. We need to find some tougher stuff to challenge those brain cells of yours. It's good to tackle harder material so you can learn to deal with frustration for later on when things don't come easy for you. And for those who struggle and don't get it: "You are really trying and I'm proud of you. You are going to master this material. Tell yourself, 'It may take a while, but I'll get it.' Let's figure out another way to look at this. I'll help you figure out what you don't understand."

These lesson plans were developed for elementary school children; however they will benefit older students and brighter children who are younger. Adults can use the ideas as well as psychology concepts remain true no matter what the age of the learner.

Some of the concepts presented here are too abstract for younger children. Of course you will need to customize the language level given in the Dialogue to meet the needs of the age of your children. Leave out the big word your children might not understand or teach the meaning of a new word. I always ask children, "Do you know what _____ means?" and then give them the definition and ask for examples from their lives. This approach gives the children time to formulate the concept into their own thinking patterns and express it in their own language. This will get the wording down to their level. If you get bewildered looks back from the children about a concept, ask them for help. I once explained a tricky concept three times to a puzzled boy changing my wording each time. Finally another boy raised his hand and said, "She means….." and gave a kid-friendly explanation. Ahhh, putting the concept into the children's own language made all the difference; everybody got it and relaxed.

Observe how the wording in the dialogues helps normalize uncomfortable feelings. Many children feel so out of control with intense feelings and think they are the only one who has felt like this. These lessons teach that it is normal to have strong feelings and then gives corrective cognitions and activities to help with them.

Children learn through repeated practice like all of us. Some of the skills are repeated in these plans with different metaphors, activities and catch words (Downer Words, Dream Stoppers, and Zombie Words). Presenting a concept in a different way with different language and different activities helps "concretize" a concept in. So pick and choose from these plans. Feel free to discard any idea that doesn't work with your group.

Choose the lesson plans that will appeal to the age and background of the children you teach. Observe which children get the lessons right away and which ones need extra attention. Motivated children catch on quickly and seem to absorb ways to become successful from their environment. Children who become discouraged easily will need your extra time and attention. Keep a close eye on them and praise them for their effort reminding them that they earned your praise.

Relational and societal poverty, neglect and trauma produce children who engage in disempowered lives creating more of that dysfunctional culture that they came from. Underneath the anger of young people lies hurt, helplessness and deep pain. The problems of many of these young people can be lessened through the efforts of many kind and caring teachers and counselors who teach a different model than was shown in the home. As this anonymous quote says so clearly.

"At the core of every problem is an issue of:
    I don't love enough.
    I am not lovable.
    I don't deserve love.
    I am unworthy.
    People cannot be trusted.

At the core of every solution:
    I am worthy and deserve love.
    I can find the peaceful solution to this.
    I love myself for I am lovable.
    I trust us to work this out by staying in love consciousness."

We can help children find their strength and see themselves as individual who can make a difference in their own lives if we emphasize growth mindsets. Our job as educators, is to help them become the best that they can be in the short time we have access to them.

As Bertha Von Suttner said, "After the verb, "To Love," "To Help" is the most beautiful verb in the world." And teaching the little ones the truth of their beauty within is a noble act of compassion. Great teachers are tough in expecting the children to do their best work but they are compassionate. Compassion is the ability to understand another person's circumstances or pain because you can see it from their point of view. Compassion as an action is the ability to reach out and care about others with kindness.

A Five to Ten Minute Investment a Day

Parents and teachers can spend five to ten minutes a day on teaching these social skills and stress management techniques. Getting your children to discuss these concepts associated with good mental health and success will enhance their self-esteem and make family relationships more loving

For many years my ongoing prayer has been, "Bless the children. Bless the teachers." You are in the front-line position to make big changes in how your children think and how they view themselves. I wish you well on your journey in understanding and teaching these important concepts that help children learn the skills that help them feel good about themselves and master their lives.

USING HELPER WORDS TO BECOME RESILIENT

<u>Objective:</u> To become aware that inner talk influences mood and behavior.

<u>Materials:</u> Rubber band.

<u>Dialogue:</u> We talk to ourselves all the time to help ourselves think and figure things out. Have you noticed that you do self-talk when you are working through a challenge? Self-talk or Helper Words are things you say to yourself that help you know what to do. You can learn positive ways to think and act by learning Helper Words. Helper Words remind you of things you can do when you are confused or upset. Use them to remember that you are in charge of your own feelings and behavior.

Resilience is staying strong and dealing with problems that come up. It is not being without problems. It is learning to deal with them through keeping a strong mind. Resilience means to be flexible, pliable like a rubber band. (Demonstrate flexibility with a rubber band.)

Resilient boys and girls keep an open mind and think in ways that make them feel like they are in control when stormy situations of life hit. How you think about things determines whether you snap under pressure. What you say in your mind tells it all. If you think you will survive, you will. If you decide you are strong and flexible, you are. Sometimes, the problem is not the real problem. The problem is how you think negatively about the problem.

Positive self-talk is crucial when you are having a tough time. Helper Words give you ideas to problem solve and discover the best thing to do. Listen to what you say to yourself when things are hard to do or you are going through a tough situation. What do you say? Do you cheer yourself on or discourage yourself? When dark storms come in, don't panic. You've handled them before and this time you are older with more experience. Here's some Helper Words some children use to problem solve and get their work done:

<u>Helper Words</u>
I keep my mind open and flexible to help solve problems.
I tell myself to slow down and take a breath when things go wrong.
I can do this. I'll keep working and figure it out.
I'm getting this figured out. I'll feel good when I'm done.

<u>Activity:</u> (Write the Helper Words on the board for the children to copy. Hand out Post It notes and ask them to write their favorite Helper Words to share with their parents and put on their mirror at home.) Let's read this list out loud. What other positive things do you say to yourself when things are tough? Which of these Helper Words do you want to remember about working with your feelings? You can feel good about yourself when you put positive Helper Words in your mind. Pat yourselves on your back when you use your Helper Words.

<u>Tips for parents and teachers:</u> The earlier these how-to-learn and stay-on-task skills that feature Helper Words are taught, the better your children's self-esteem will become. Competence equals believing in yourself and knowing that you can handle stress and new and challenging tasks. Children need to learn to feel competent before the onset of adolescence sets in with its hormonal and neurochemical changes along with risky behaviors.

Stuff happens.

Sometimes bad stuff happens.

We all have tough times in life.

Tough times require your finding your courage and getting tougher.

Being resilient is getting back up after you fall.

Hang calm; take a deep breath and yell,

"I use my Helper Words.
"I will get through this. I will survive!"

Clip art © www.djinkers.com

BOUNCE BACK TO BECOME RESILIENT

<u>Objective</u>: To become stronger and more capable of dealing with life's hardships.

<u>Materials</u>: Weebles (an oval shaped figure that pops back up when knocked down. A two pack of Playskool Weebles costs around $8.00.)

<u>Dialogue</u>: Resilience is the ability to bounce back after a fall. Being a resilient person means to rebound, to come back to a positive position and recover your strength. Resilience means that you spring back and don't let unhappy experiences keep you down.

Hardships are part of life. You might feel caught in troubles, troubles and more troubles. Too many troubles and too many bad feelings can pull you into a downward spiral. You can be a "sit down and do nothing except feel sorry for yourself kind of person" or you can be a go getter.

<u>Activity</u>: Bouncing Back when Knocked Over. These Weebles know how to get back up when they are knocked down. They don't stay down and feel sorry for themselves. They bounce back up fast. (Pass the Weebles around so the children can experience them.)

Remember Bozo, the punching bag clown who bounces back when knocked down? The harder he is punched, the more he bounces back. He is resilient and can't be knocked down for good. See what you can learn about bouncing back when things go wrong from this video.

<u>Activity</u>: Watch the Bounce Back Kid cartoon on YouTube at www.youtube.com/watch?v=eVTO1nIK7CA or on my web site at http://www.angriesout.com/bounceback/bbkid3.swf listed under Interactive Videos.

Stress and setbacks happen to all of us. Have you ever felt pressured and trapped like the boy in the video? Have you ever been so wound up you felt like you might snap? What makes you feel stressed? What types of life events might make someone feel upset? Tell us about a time when you were a Bounce Back Kid.

When your life is on the line, keep your attitude bright and you will keep moving forward. Keep trying stuff. Try another way if the first way you try doesn't work. You are tougher than you think. You are smarter and stronger than you realize. Nothing is over until you give up. Push yourself to the limit and you will be surprised at how tough you are. Anything is possible if you've got the courage to get 'er done." Build a good track record for getting through tough times. Hardships often prepare you for an extraordinary destiny.

<u>Helper Words:</u>
Bad times and hardships are not going to knock me down.
If I get punched down, I jump back up.
Stress heading my way? I'm ready to be bouncable!
Got bounce? YESSS! I AM THE BOUNCE BACK KID!

<u>Tips for parents and teachers:</u> Believe in the resiliency of your children. Notice when they are under stress. Remind them of the possibility of their becoming a confident person: "See yourself becoming how you want to be. Remind yourself that you are a person who can pull your own weight. Talk to yourself about becoming a strong person who can handle hard times because you believe in yourself."

Resilience is knowing that
you will be okay no matter
what happens.

Resilience puts you in charge.

Resilience happens when
you use your Helper Words.

You never know how strong you are until
you are forced with a challenge.

Then being strong is the
only choice you have!

BECOMING A HARDY PERSON

Objective: To feel proud about being a tough, hardy person.

Dialogue: Have you heard the saying "When the going gets tough, the tough get hardy?" What does that mean? What is tough or difficult for you? What hard things do you have to face or deal with that makes you feel challenged and tested? (Sympathize with each child who volunteers saying something like, "Whew! That *is* a challenge." Don't go into problem solving—the goal here is to get him or her to believe in themselves and tackle their own problem.)

The word "hardy" comes from the word "hard." (Point to some things that are hard like the floor, a desk, etc. Write the word hard and hardy on the board.) People who do hard things become hardy. When times are tough, we have to find the courage to deal with it and tackle it head on. The definition of courage is facing your fear and going right through it.

If hardy people take a hit or fall down, they bounce back up. The harder you fall, the bigger you can bounce. You can make yourself bouncable! Learning to bounce back when something hard happens to you prepares you to deal with anything that comes along.

Activity: Sing along with the Bounce Back song on YouTube by Frank Servello at http://www.youtube.com/watch?v=RKN2KEHn5dk.

Activity: Color the Resilience poster. Draw a picture of yourself bouncing back after being knocked down using some of the bounce back pictures.

Allow challenges in your life. If it doesn't challenge you, it doesn't change you. You have some strengths to draw from. Act hardy and you will become a hardy person. Tell yourself that things will get better and keep working at it so they do get better. Give yourself a pep talk: "Today, I will be hardy. No matter what happens, I will be tough, strong and resilient. I choose to be dynamic and strong. I tell myself I am quick to recover from unfortunate things. I am the Bounce Back Kid!"

Helper Words:
 I am resilient when troubles and problems come at me.
 I challenge troubles by doing the best I can.
 I stop feeling sorry for myself and start to do something.
 Awesome. I tell myself that I'll do the best I can and that is awesome!

PROBLEMS OVERCOME MAKE YOU A STRONGER PERSON

<u>Objective:</u> To learn from adversity and become a stronger, wiser person.

<u>Dialogue:</u> There's something good about getting hard knocks in life. Unhappy events can be lessons to learn from and get through. Tough things happen but you are tougher than they are. Problems can make you stronger if you learn to deal with them. They can help you learn to overcome failure by getting back up and having another go at what you are facing. Overcoming a problem helps you gain positive coping skills to deal with tougher times. When you are stuck in a bad situation try to learn something new about yourself.

<u>Activity:</u> Let's watch a You Tube video on keeping a positive attitude at http://www.mentormob.com/learn/i/positive-messages-growth-mindsets/youtube-best-motivation-video-ever

<u>Discussion Questions:</u>
Tell of a time you learned an important life lesson from going through a hard time.
What did you learn about yourself when you went through a rough time?
What important feedback did you receive that you didn't like about yourself but you knew that it was true.
What lesson are you learning about yourself right now?
What can you say during a crisis to make yourself strong and hardy??

Acknowledge your good points and keep challenging any habits that you know are not good for you. Keep reminding yourself, "These are my values and this is what I stand for." Remember to keep an open mind so that new information can come in. An open mind gives you all kinds of new possibilities. Ask yourself, "How can I see this differently and learn something new?" Then you can give yourself a pat on the back and say, "Wow, that's awesome. I learned something new from this and that is awesome."

<u>Helper Words:</u>
I count! I deserve to feel good about myself and my life.
Happy by choice today! I make good choices and keep my mind happy.
When I fix my thinking, my problems can solve themselves.
I make it real. With my positive thoughts, nothing can keep me down!

The Okays about Feelings for Kids of All Ages:

It is okay for you to feel any way you feel.
It is not okay to take bad feelings out on others.
It is okay for your feelings to change.
It is okay to feel sad and angry when you hurt.
It is okay to feel confused if you don't understand.
It is okay to feel scary inside.
It is okay to cry when you are hurting.
It is okay to ask for help.
It is okay to ask for a hug or to be held.
It is necessary for you to take care of yourself.
It's necessary that you learn to calm yourself down.
It's not okay to act out your feelings when upset.
It is most certainly okay for you to be yourself.
It is okay for you to be who you are."

GIVE YOURSELF PERMISSION TO HAVE FEELINGS

<u>Objective</u>: To learn about and accept all feelings that make us human.

<u>Materials</u>: The chart, *The Okays About Feelings for Kids of all Ages*.

<u>Dialogue</u>: We are people with feelings. Feelings are sad, mad, glad, bad, disappointed, confused, lost, rejected, happy, grumpy, neglected, etc. When you say, "I feel like running or going home… (doing something) is not a feeling. That is an action you want to take. Saying "I feel discouraged" is a real feeling. You can use your feelings and your body to let people know about you.

<u>Activity</u>: Watch and discuss the video, Saying What You Mean - A Children's Book about Communication Skills by Joy Wilt. http://www.youtube.com/watch?v=1hnLfnulwZw

<u>Activity</u>: Being Okay About the Okays. Let's practice on naming REAL feelings and list them on the board. (Discuss the concepts given in the chart that give children permission to have feelings and be who they are. Have the children read the ideas out loud in unison. Ask the children to generate examples of each of the Okays. Give them copies and have them draw a border around the words repeating their name around the edge of the paper. Build a strong association between speaking uncomfortable feelings and getting relief from them. Have the children memorize this poem by chanting it out loud several times together.)

Feelings come and feelings go.
Some are fast and some are slow!
When I am down and feel so low,
I talk about them and to let them go!

Sharing feelings helps you feel better but choose wisely who you share with. You can't share your deepest feelings with everyone. Some people cannot hear about your feelings. They feel threatened and get upset and angry. Some will tell others what you said and gossip about you. Feelings are tender and are to be treated with respect. Share your feelings with kind and loving people who handle them gently.

<u>Teacher Cues</u>
Tell yourself, "I'm a talk-about-my-feelings kind of person."
You don't have to hold on to bad feelings; find someone and talk them out.
You are a better person for learning how to deal with your feelings.
Talk to him. Go over and tell him how you felt when he grabbed your paper.

<u>Helper Words for Children:</u>
Feelings come and go. I can let bad feelings go when I talk about them.
I don't need to hold onto my bad feelings.
I can find someone safe to talk to when I feel upset.
I can make good choices and take care of myself.

<u>Tips for parents and teachers:</u> Group rituals bond the children laying the foundation for positive social change within your classroom or family. Group rehearsals via chanting are very effective in memorization of these positive messages. Doing things together at the same time with other people bonds and expands our sense of self, according to research. Chanting or repeating out loud the Helper Words gives auditory cues that help implant them in your children's mind.

"You and only you are the designer
and developer of your life.

You are in control of a large
part of your destiny.

At times, you are held back
by your fears.

To walk into the storm of conflict
with head bowed and the
determination to see where
it takes you so that the issue
may be dealt with is courage.

Courage is facing
short-term discomfort
to gain long-term peace."

Lynne Namka

WORK IT OUT OR ACT IT OUT

<u>Objective</u>: To recognize and name feelings.

<u>Dialogue</u>: Unhappy and angry feelings are normal when something bad happens. Too often we learn to stuff them down because they are uncomfortable. But then feelings get bogged down and pile up and bust out when we don't want them to. It is normal to have strong feelings when you have been hurt or when something went wrong. It's what you do with your feelings that count. They are just feelings to be felt and then do something with. When you are angry would it be better to work angry feelings out or act them out?

<u>Activity</u>: Finding and Busting Stuck Feelings: Think of something that troubled you recently. Name a feeling about it. Feel a piece of it and tell yourself it is just a feeling. Find where your body feels tense. Instead of acting on it, just stay with it. Feelings are meant to be felt. That's why they are called feelings. You bust them when you call them out to deal with them. Some feelings like to hide underground. Feeling go away faster when you call them out and give them a name. The first thing to do when you are upset is to notice your feeling. Then name your feeling. Name it and tame it!

Sometimes feelings stack up and hide underneath each other. You can break down a big feeling like anger to see what other emotions might be lurking underneath. There is no set pattern. Hurt and sadness might be hiding under anger. Anger might be hiding under fear and confusion. Find the emotion that is on top and work on releasing it, then ask yourself what other feelings you might have. As you address each feeling, the whole stack of feelings might start to shift.

Uncomfortable feelings can decrease when you face them. Say your feeling out loud so you can deal with it. For example if you are afraid of snakes and see a pet snake you might say, "That snake is terrifying, but it is so beautiful. I wonder how it feels. I'll touch it:" Challenging your fear can reduce it. If you run away from fear, it comes with you.

So feelings it is! Feelings are meant to be felt; that's why they are called feelings. If you are a human being, you most certainly have feelings. Put your uncomfortable feelings on notice. Tell them that you are busting them. Make a new rule for yourself: "If I feel it, I own it. I get honest with myself. I can work this out or I can act it out." If I spot it, I got it! I'll breathe into it and talk it out."

<u>Helper Words</u>
I recognize unhappy feelings and do something about them.
I'm putting this feeling on notice that I'm on to it. I call it out to be understood.
I'll work my bad feelings out so I don't have to act them out.
It's only a feeling. I tell myself, "Let's do this!"

Five Rules about Feelings

1. Call them out and name and tame them.

2. Tolerate them. They are just feelings after all.

3. Learn tools to send unwanted ones packing.

4. Take charge and soothe your own bad feelings.

5. You are a human being with feelings and that's a marvelous thing to be!

Lynne Namka   Teaching Emotional Intelligence to Children

©dianne j. hook

THE SADS TECHNIQUE: SOOTHE AWAY DISTRESS AND SADNESS

Objective: To learn two simple ways to release unhappy feelings.

Dialogue: Everyone gets sad sometimes. Sadness is about a loss of some kind. Your mind is like a computer. You can reprogram your mind to release unhappy feelings. Tapping and stretching your eyes put information in different parts of the brain. The lung meridian holds the energies of sadness. When you tap this meridian, finding a tender or a sore spot means you have a block in the lung meridian.

Activity: Think about the thing that makes you feel unhappy. How sad are you? A little, some or quite a bit? Show me by putting your hands out in front of you to show your amount of sadness.

Start tapping briskly on the outside of your thumb beside your fingernail. Slowly tap from the outside of your thumb up the inside of your arm, across your shoulder and then down your chest where the strap of a t-shirt would be. Think of what you are sad about and look for a sore spot.

Tap on the sore spot and breathe deeply and think about sadness. See if a memory is there behind that sore spot and breathe into it. Just accept that you become sad when you have been hurt or you lose something. Tap on the sore spot until it goes away. Tap on your other arm from your thumb to your chest to find other sore spots.

Now check your sadness level. Are you still sad a little, some or a lot? Make fists and cross your arms making an X on your chest. Pound on your chest two inches above the inside your armpits.

Tap on the side of your hand just below your little finger. Say out loud three times, "I love and accept myself even though I'm sad.

Activity: Chase More Sad Feelings Away With the "Eyes Up and Down Technique." Are you still sad? You are a good person even if you have sad feelings. Tap briskly on the back of the web of your hand between your ring finger and little finger. Think about how you feel hurt and sad. You are a normal human being with feelings and that is an okay way to be when you've been hurt or lose something important. Forgive yourself for having normal emotions of feeling hurt and sad.

Hold your head level and lower your eyes to look down at the floor. Slowly raise your eyes to the ceiling without moving your head. Roll your eyes in a big circle from the floor to the ceiling and take a breath and then roll your eyes the opposite direction.

Do you really need to hold onto sadness? Breathe in and out and let your sad feelings go. Send them away by blowing them out. If your sadness goes away, you have released the energy behind it! If the sadness is still there, repeat the steps or find a safe person to process your loss or keep doing these tapping procedures to work the issue.

Helper Words:
Feelings come and feelings go. I can let my feelings go.
I tap and breathe to let unhappy feelings go.
Life is tough sometimes but so am I so I work with my feelings.
I am a person with feelings and that is a marvelous thing to be.

WRITING TO CLEAR ANGRY FEELINGS

<u>Objective:</u> Releasing feelings by writing about them.

<u>Dialogue:</u> We all have problems; it is what we do with them that count. Feelings about a problem come up to get you to pay attention to them. Anger may mean that someone has hurt your feelings. Sadness may mean that you have lost something important and are trying to deal with it. Talk to your stuck feeling. Listen to what it has to say. Is there hurt or sadness hiding underneath the anger?

<u>Activity:</u> Sometimes feelings get blocked. Stuck feelings want to move. Writing about angry feelings can help get the problem out of your mind and down on the computer screen or paper in black and white. Writing about your feelings helps you see things more clearly as it forces you to see what you are doing. Writing things down helps clarify and release feelings. Do not text or send them! It's for your private use only. Tear this up when you are done or delete it from your computer.

1. "My Feelings Wants to be Written Down!" Use a dark crayon or a big, bold font when writing this about your anger and be as mad as you want. Note how anger takes over your body and mind. Do some deep breathing to make yourself feel better.Keep your writing short. Stick to your feelings: "I felt angry when _____. I felt hurt when _____."

2. "The I'm Getting Clearer!" Write again about your same feelings. This time use dark ink or a smaller computer font. Check your assumptions as to what you believe about how another person has tried to harm you. No matter what happened, you are responsible for what happens to you now and you want to move on. You want to make your mind clear.

3. "Words from the Heart." Focus on your angry, hurt or sad feeling. Drop into your heart. Now breathe into it and think about your future. Do you want to continue with these unhappy feelings? What does your heart want to happen? It wants peace for you. Think about peace while you breathe deeply and let your anger go.

<u>Helper Words</u>
Why am I angry about this? How have I been hurt or threatened?
I look under my anger to see if hurt or sadness are hiding there.
Unhappy feelings can be released when I write about them.
Feelings want to move. They come and go. I let unhappy feelings go.

<u>Tips for parents and teachers:</u> Fantasy writers and horror movie makers know that before you can kill the monster, you must say its name out loud! Start naming feelings out loud yourself for your children to overhear, "I give myself one-hundred percent permission to call out unhappy feelings by name." Emotional Intelligence skills are easy to teach children once you have the basic understanding of the nuts and bolts of dealing with feelings. More skills for coping with feelings are taught in my companion book called *Teaching Emotional Intelligence to Children.*

Have a Gratitude Attitude!

What are you grateful for?

Look inside your heart.

Take deep breaths.

Think of something you are grateful for.

Think of another thing. And another thing.

I am grateful for

_____

_____

_____

_____

Every day can be gratitude day!

Make Gratitude a year-round Attitude!

Clip art © www.djinkers.com

THE SECRET OF SUCCESS

<u>Objective:</u> To equate success and doing well in life with effort.

<u>Dialogue:</u> People who do well in life know that success results from small efforts done day in and day out. Giving good effort has two rewards: (1.) you will be successful and (2.) you will feel good about yourself.

Do you have a "Give Up" part of yourself that convinces you to stop working when you have a hard job to do? New things like the multiplication tables or hitting a ball can be hard to learn at first. What are some things that you found hard to learn? What did you have to do to get it mastered? Different people have different things that they find hard to learn at first. That's okay.

People who feel good about themselves and have good self-esteem get that way because they feel competent. Competent means that they have learned skills and do what it takes to get the job done. People who learn to do something new can get a boost in feeling good. But if you give up and stop trying, you are putting a roadblock in your way and don't get the new skill learned. Then you might feel bad about yourself.

Once you get a new skill learned, really learned well, you will have it the rest of your life. The difference between people who don't well and those who do is effort and practice. Trying hard and keeping your eye on the goal gets the job done. Make the job much easier by telling yourself that you are going to get it.

<u>Activity:</u> What do you think success is? What do you have to do to become successful? Let's watch movie actor Will Smith talk about his success about working hard to get what he wants. No roadblocks for him! He says he is successful because he works harder than other people.

http://www.mentormob.com/learn/i/positive-messages-growth-mindsets/youtube-will-smith-mindset

There will be many distractions that will take you away from achieving your goal. There will be people who will try to divert you away by asking you to do risky activities. That's the time when you have to put your foot down and say, "I'd rather not. I got important stuff to do" and give a firm, clear NO. You might feel bad for a moment but think of how good you will feel when your hard work pays off and you get your goal.

<u>Helper Words:</u>
I can feel good about myself for putting in the effort.
I use my Helper Words to blast through any roadblocks.
I tell myself "Woah! High praise for hard work!"
Success is getting through a challenging task, putting in the work and feeling good.

<u>Tips for parents and teachers:</u> Asking for help is a necessary skill for life success. Children need to learn the skills to advocate for themselves so they can navigate job hunting, social agencies and organizations in the real world. One study found that working-class parents coached their children on how to avoid problems and to be deferential to authority figures. Middle-class parents were more likely to encourage their kids to speak up and ask questions or ask for help.

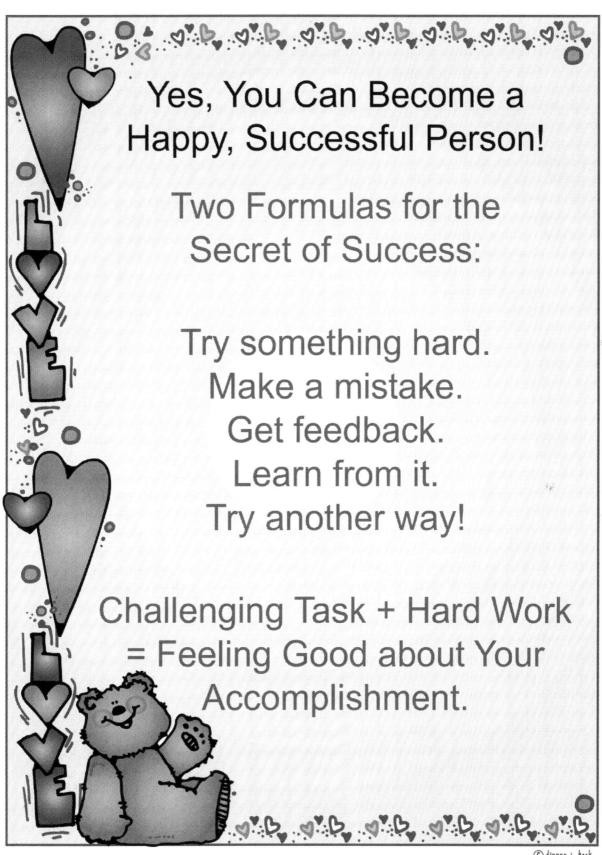

Yes, You Can Become a
Happy, Successful Person!

Two Formulas for the
Secret of Success:

Try something hard.
Make a mistake.
Get feedback.
Learn from it.
Try another way!

Challenging Task + Hard Work
= Feeling Good about Your
Accomplishment.

© dianne j. hook

FEEL PROUD AND PRAISE YOURSELF WHEN YOU WORK REALLY HARD

<u>Objective:</u> To learn to use self-praise with discretion.

<u>Dialogue:</u> You know when you have put in extra effort or not. If you tell yourself, "Good job" when you haven't worked hard, you are lying to yourself. That is false praise. It is junk praise. If you praise yourself too much for easy tasks, it backfires on you because it's not sincere.

<u>Activity:</u> Think of a time when you learned something hard and wanted to give up. Remember how good you felt after you got it mastered. Remember the feeling of winning a race or a game when you put extra effort in and it was worth it. Think about how you felt when you worked through something you didn't think you could do. Got it? That's the feeling of pride. You can feel proud when you did something you didn't know that you could do. Think of another time you did extraordinary work. Remember how satisfied and pleased you felt about pushing yourself through a bad time? That's a time to congratulate yourself with self-praise. You don't want to be a praise junky expecting to get constant attention for your work.

You can build self-confidence through hard work and preparation. Praise yourself when you have done something that you worked hard on and feel proud. Let's do some fun types of self-praise. Think about something hard you are learning now. Think of how you will feel when you get it learned. Then do one of these awesome self praise actions:

High Fives.   Fist Bumps.
Patting yourself on the shoulder.   Tell yourself "Fannnntastic!"
A-Okay sign.   Fists in the air with a "Yessss!"
Give yourself a big bear hug.

Notice how you feel alive and excited after accomplishing something important. Are there any other words and actions that you do to cheer yourself on? Which ones do you like best?

What you do every day matters. Success is not a once-in-a-while thing—it's applying determination daily to build the habit of being a winner. Day by day, you build habits and character. Doing your work even if you don't feel like it and daily getting the habit of getting down to work with that "git er done" habit makes you successful at whatever you choose to do!

<u>Helper Words:</u>
I'll give myself a pat on the back for working really hard.
I feel satisfied when I push myself to learn something new.
Woo. Hoo! I got it done. It was hard but I did it.
Finishing something challenging makes me feel proud.

<u>Tips for parents and teachers:</u> Your saying "Good job!" to your child when he or she has not done anything extraordinary will cause him to avoid applying himself. Praise only when it is really deserved and then for the hard work put in *and* for positive characteristics *not talent or intelligence*. For example, "Your grades show that you have really worked hard and I really like the person you are!"

Life is about failure as much as it is about success.

When you make a mistake, keep your self esteem and admit you goofed up.

When you work hard and succeed, give yourself a big Attaboy or Attagirl!

Remember to praise yourself when you do something really big, not for the small stuff.

The more you succeed and praise yourself for your effort, the easier it becomes.

High Fives.
Fist Bumps.
Pat yourself on the shoulder.
Fannnntastic!
A-Okay sign.
Fists in the air with a "Yessss!"
Give yourself a big bear hug.

USE YOUR IMAGINATION TO CHANGE THE MEANING OF THE PROBLEM!

<u>Objective</u>: To experience cognitive reappraisal and how stepping back and observing a problem from a different perspective can decrease emotion.

<u>Dialogue</u>: Sometimes your mind is not your friend. It tries to frighten you for no good reason. Fear thoughts can take a situation and make it seem much worse. It can paint an ugly picture of what might happen.

<u>Activity:</u> Let's play *Backwards Mother May I?* by using your imagination. (Line the children up and explain the *Mother May I* game). Think about something that bothers you. Try this step-back approach to create some distance from what bothers you by taking a picture of it and making it smaller. Close your eyes and use your imagination to see the situation that bothers you. Pretend that you take a picture of it with an imaginary camera.

Let's play Mother May I? You say, "Mother, may I take a tiny, huge or giant step back from my problem?" If I say, "Yes, you may," you get to step back. But if I just say "Yes" you don't get to step back and have to stay where you are." Ask me if you can step back from your problem and let's practice listening for the "Yes, you may."

Take your fearful or angry feelings with you as you step back. Now take two giant steps back and let your feelings fade. Keep stepping back until the situation is a tiny picture far away from you. Be curious as you observe it. Step away from the problem, Ma'am or Sir. Just step away!

You can't always change what happens to you. But you can change how you see the troublesome situation. You can change how you think about it. You can change the "Oh, no, this is terrible" to "I can handle this."

Notice your situation now. Does it look any different? Are you more in charge? Ask yourself, "How could I see this differently? I'm in charge of my mind and how I see things. How could I change my mind about this? How can I see it differently so it might come out better? Change it up. Walk around that problem and look at it from a 360 degree view. See what upsets you from a faraway place. Pretend that you could climb a tree or a mountain or go up to the roof of a tall building and look down on your problem.

Change your direction of your thinking if you get stuck. Try, try again and see your problem from a different angle. When things don't go right, go left!

My Plan for Change

Change, change, change will do me good!

What area of my life am I'm unhappy about?

What would someone who cares about me advise me to do about this?

Why do I want change this behavior?

What excuses have I been telling myself to keep myself from moving forward?

How do I distract myself away from taking positive action?

What fears do I have about making this change?

What beliefs do I have that create huge obstacles in my mind?

What is in it for me to start this change process?

What is the first step that I could take? Can I imagine myself doing this step?

Am I willing to do that first step and see what happens?

What is the best thing that will happen if I make this change?

USE YOUR IMAGAINATION TO MAKE A MOVIE IN YOUR MIND

<u>Objective:</u> To imagine a different outcome to a problem.

<u>Activity:</u> Watch Your Movie that You Made Up. Close your eyes and turn on your wild imagination. Put a situation that disturbs your mind on a large picture screen. You are the writer, director and actor of a story about your problem. You just watch rather than reacting. Set your feelings aside, just observe you story. You use your mind to create new possibilities for yourself by writing a movie and giving it a different ending.

Sit watching the movie screen from the front of a movie theater as your story unfolds. You have different parts of yourself that can watch the movie from different parts of the theater. The first part of you sits in the front row. A second part of you sits in the middle of the theater and watches the part of you that sits in front watching the picture on the screen. Then make another part of you that sits in the back of the theater that observes you in the middle watching you in the front studying you on the screen. Take another part of you that sits in the balcony watching you in the back of the theater watching you in the middle watching you in the front watching you on the screen. You are you, watching you, watching you, watching you watch the screen!

How would you like your movie to end? You are the writer of your movie; you can change the script anytime. Make the ending into a happy one. Turn yourself into a superhero or invite a superhero to come in and help you. Paint a clear picture in your mind and see yourself succeeding.

<u>Activity:</u> Practice, practice, practice this game of stepping back and observing from a faraway place rather than reacting with intense emotions. Practice makes permanent. Practice your strengths and they will become stronger. Let's watch this video of three-year-old Beyonce dancing. When she was little, she sang and practiced harder than the other girls at singing and dancing. And she became a star.
http://www.youtube.com/watch?v=bzfrKaPamn4

<u>Helper Words</u>
What is my goal here? How can I imagine it differently?
What is another way of looking at this?
What am I missing? What am I not seeing?
How would the wisest person I know think about this?

Use your creative imagination to set your mind to have a happy successful life.

Believe that you can grow
and learn and you can!

When you slip into distractive thinking,
reel your mind back in.

Imagine yourself trying hard and winning.
See yourself as a winner.
Feel the good feeling of success.

Create a mindset of winning!

SELF SOOTHING: MAKING YOURSELF FEEL GOOD

Objective: To learn self-calming touch techniques.

Materials: A variety of soft and smooth tactile objects and fabrics such as silk, felt, flannel, velvet and fur that feel good on the skin and different types of plastic and wood self massage tools.

Dialogue: What did you do when you were little to feel secure and safe? Did you hold on to your blanket or suck on a pacifier or your thumb. What do you do now when you are feeling insecure to take care of yourself? (Ideas include holding a favorite stuffed animal or gaining comfort from a pet, rocking, taking a warm bath or listening to music.) You can learn to soothe or calm yourself.

Activity: Our skin is the largest organ in the body. The skin receives certain types of touch which can be soothing. Scratching, touching and massage release the good chemicals in the brain to help people feel better. These positive brain chemicals are called endorphins and can be activated by stimulating the scalp and skin. Let's do a Knuckle Rub on your scalp to see if that makes you feel better. (Demonstrate how rubbing the head and the temples feel good.) Massaging your arms and legs can calm you. Brushing your hair can stimulate you. Back scratching feels good. Your body likes touch. Do you like a light touch or a deep touch?

See which of these objects and fabrics feel good to your skin. Learn natural ways to calm your body so you don't have to turn to things outside yourself to feel better such as eating or using alcohol or drugs. Find what calming activities work for you and do more of them. (Suggest that there are different activities that could be substituted for nail biting such as rolling a marble in the hands or tucking the thumb into the other fingers while breathing deeply.)

Helper Words:
I can tap, rub and massage my body to feel better.
I learn what kinds of things make my body relaxed.
I learn and use many techniques to calm myself.
Self-soothing makes me feel better and wakes up the happy chemicals in my brain.

Tips for parents and teachers: Watch your child when he or she is stressed to see if they revert back to bad habits of eating or too much television or video games. When you notice your children are in a bad mood, ask them to do twenty fist bumps reaching high over their heads while saying "Yes! Yes! Yes! with each bump. If a child does not decrease his mood after completing these two exercises as shown by the distance between his or her hands, there may be a deeper issue that needs intervention with you or a counselor.

Calm yourself with self-soothing.

Tap and rub your body.

Take deep breaths to reset
your brain.

Stay away from that Panic Button.

Think before you act;
not act before you think.

Give yourself positive pep talks.

Tell yourself, "I'm strong. I will get
through this.

I will endure.

I will survive!"

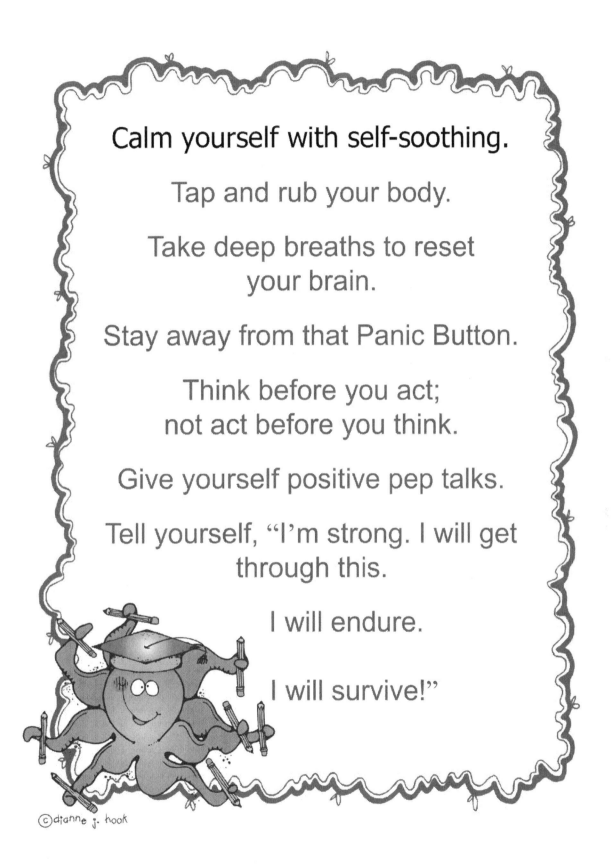

©dianne j. hook

PUT YOUR WORRIES IN PERSPECTIVE

Objective: To learn ideas and techniques that decrease anxiety.

Dialogue: Everybody has problems. Some problems are real and need to be dealt with. Other times your mind makes up unnecessary problems to worry about. Watch how your mind grabs onto worry thoughts and makes you miserable. Too many worry thoughts can stress you out and become your enemy. Worry thoughts try to trick you in to feeling overwhelmed and wear you out. Then you might fall back into bad habits.

Activity: Let's list some things children worry about on the board: (Parent's fighting, fear of a hard test, best friend moving away, being bullied, sick family members, etc.) Constant worrying about something that is happening to you creates anxiety. When you worry about something that you can't change, you stress yourself out. These are Unhelpful Worries.

There is another kind of worry that actually helps you if you do it correctly. Worry can have a positive purpose. It helps you to notice something that might need change. The helpful kind of worry reminds you to get a plan for what you want to happen. For example, if you worry about your grades, you could plan to study and do better. If you are worried about your little brother acting out, you could talk to someone about getting help for him. So a little bit of worry of the Get a Plan type can actually help you.

Let's go back to those Unhelpful Worries that you can't change that keep your mind in turmoil. Let's listen to Bob Marley's happy song which has a "lighten up" message for you:

http://www.youtube.com/watch?v=mACqcZZwG0k

Correct your worry thought by calling it out, giving it a name and challenge it by telling it to go away. Turn it around and think of the best thing that could happen. Stop worrying about what could go wrong and think of one thing that could go right. Now think of another thing. And another thing. Get excited about what might happen for the best.

Music can be calming and energizing at the same time.

Helper Words:
I use my worry to get a plan to deal with my problem and then let it go.
If plan A doesn't work, there are 25 more letters in the alphabet.
I stop thinking about what could go wrong and think of what could go right.
Is my worry the kind I need to let go of or get a plan for?

"Hang tough when things get rough.

Hang strong when things go wrong."

PUTTING YOUR WORRIES SOMEWHERE SAFE

Objective: To turn worry over to the unconscious mind for release.

Materials: Smooth rocks, gemstones, sea glass and a small cardboard box.

Dialogue: Many of our worries are about terrible things that we think might happen. This is called making a mountain out of a molehill. Sometimes the worry thoughts in the mind go to the worst thing that could happen. Then we get stuck on that. When you notice that you are worrying too much about something that you have no control over, use your wonderful imagination. You can imagine putting your unnecessary worries somewhere safe. You can put your worries in a Worry Stone or in a Worry Box.

Activity: Putting Unhelpful Worries in a Worry Stone or Worry Box. Pretend that your Worry Stone can absorb your unhappy thoughts. Look for a smooth rock that has been tumbled by friction of being rolled by water or the earth or tumbled gem stone that can become your Worry Stone. The rock has been worried by the earth or water so it knows how to take your worries so you don't have to carry them with you.

If you can't find a smooth stone, make a Worry Box to put your worries into. Make it a real box or an imaginary one. Write the bad situation down on a piece of paper and put it in the Worry Box. Let's make some designs and write out some Helper Words to decorate our box. I'll cut a slot in the top for the worries to slip through. Write down some worries to put in our Worry Box.

You can make a Worry Box at home. Put an imaginary lock on it and store it on the highest shelf in your house. You can take that box down and look at your worry for a few minutes if you want to but don't do it too often. Every time you look at the worry say, "I'm in charge of you and you have to shrink down." After a while make it shrink away forever using your imagination. If it pops back up, tell it "I'm too busy. I have no time for worry."

Helper Words:
I'm in charge of what goes on in my mind.
I banish unhelpful worries.
I watch my mind and talk to it when I get upset with myself.
Unhelpful worry thoughts get out of my mind!

Tips for parents and teachers: Notice the sensitive, lonely, withdrawn and acting out children who need an encouraging word from you. You can make a difference with children who give up early. Research showed that black seventh graders improved their performance when they had a teacher who conveyed high standards and believed they could reach the high goals. We all need a wise teacher like that. I was such an awkward, shy klutchy kid who had several teachers who took a special interest in me and that helped shape me into the person I am today. How about you?

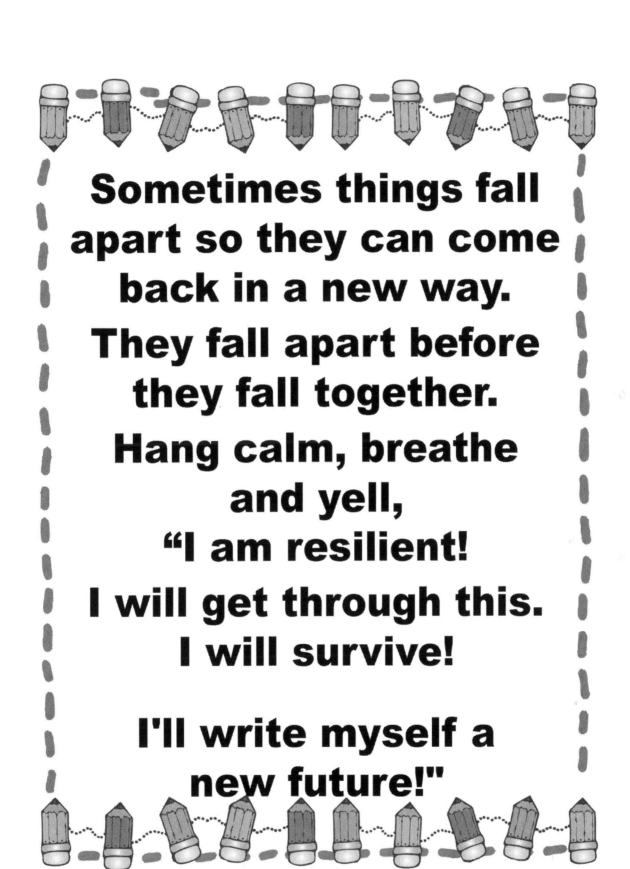

Sometimes things fall apart so they can come back in a new way.
They fall apart before they fall together.
Hang calm, breathe and yell,
"I am resilient!
I will get through this.
I will survive!

I'll write myself a new future!"

©dianne j. hook

WALK, TALK, HUFF AND PUFF TO CHASE BAD FEELINGS AWAY

<u>Objective:</u> To experience release of tension through moving the big muscles and breathing.

<u>Dialogue:</u> What is stress? There are two kinds. Outside stressors are the unhappy events that happen to you. Inside stress is the pressure, strain and worry that you put on yourselves when something bad has happened. Then you might get in a crabby mood. Bad moods are contagious just like the flu. You can catch a bad mood from being around grouchy, grumpy people. It doesn't take much to put you in a bad mood. Bad moods zap your energy and slow down your thinking. They have a multiplier effect—they make everything seem worse.

When you are stressed, choose something positive to do. Stressed people sometimes fall back on their own bad habits. Sitting on the couch or lying in bed and watching television are some of the worst things to do when you feel grumpy, anxious or sorry for yourself. Avoid eating too much, doing excessive video games, hurting your body or turning to risky activities. Make an effort to talk to a friend, listen to music, play an instrument, go for a walk, run, bike ride, read a book, play catch or shoot hoops.

When you are upset, notice where your body feels tense. Tension is a signal that your muscles need stretching and movement. Doing something to move your body can help chase away stressful anxious feelings. Exercise causes your brain to release those feel-good chemicals. Moving your big muscles and breathing helps alter brain chemistry. Things don't seem so bad and you'll feel happier after doing some vigorous activity.

<u>Activity:</u> Walk, Talk, Huff and Puff. Think of a bad mood you have had lately. (Show with your hands held apart the size how big a bad mood might be.) Is it small, medium or gigantic? When your body feels tight or restless when you are stressed, it's telling you it is time to get up and stretch and move around! It is saying "Move me. Move me. Move that ol' bod!" Exercise such as playing ball, walking and dancing increase blood circulation in your body which releases stress. Physical activity reorganizes your brain and boosts your learning and memory. Movement helps particularly when you are learning a hard task.

Let's go outside do the Walk, Talk, Huff and Puff routine. Let's walk briskly around the playground while we huff and puff and breathe deeply. (Say "I can't hear you! I can't hear you breathing." in a deep funny voice to get the children making more noise with their breath which indicates taking deeper breaths.)

Think about the bad mood now and show me how big it is now. Using positive Helper Words while you move your body chases bad moods away even faster. Which Helper Words are you going to use to knock that bad mood out of the park?

<u>Helper Words:</u>
I chase bad moods away through deep breathing and moving my body.
I pay attention to the message behind stressful feelings and body tension.
I release tension through exercise.
I take action. Walk, talk, huff and puff makes me feel better.

How you feel about yourself affects
everything you do.

Tell yourself what you need to hear
to shift your mood.

Shift gears into the Positive.

Make the right decisions,
not the easy ones.

Throw out those old
"defeat-yourself" words.

Pull out those bad feelings and
send them packing.

Give yourself permission
to feel gooooood!

PULLING OUT BAD FEELINGS

<u>Objective</u>: To use the imagination and visualization to release bad feelings.

<u>Dialogue</u>: Sometimes feelings get stuck because you don't know that they are there or don't know how to let them go. You can learn many techniques to work with your feelings and release them. Remember unhappy feelings can get stuck but stuck feelings want to move. They come up to remind you to do something about them. You don't need to hold onto unwelcome feelings. There are many different things that you can do with them.

<u>Activity</u>: Pull Outs. Pull Outs add action to your imagination by pretending to take away an uncomfortable feeling you don't want. Think of an unhappy feeling. Now feel it. Where does it hide in your body? Is it in your stomach, chest, shoulders, hands or legs? It might feel like a tight place or somewhere your body feels uncomfortable.

Remember it's only a feeling! What color is the feeling? How big is it? Let the feeling get stronger and stronger. Double it now; now make the feeling worse. Do you like this feeling? Do you want to keep that unhappy feeling? Okay now, what do you want to do with it? Pretend that you can pull it out. Reach down and start to pull it out. Use your hands to grab it and pull it out and throw it away. Pull it up and pull it out and throw it in the trash! (Demonstrate finding an anxious feeling in your stomach and pulling it out and throwing it away in the trash.)

<u>Activity</u>: Where You Gonna Send Bad Feelings? Your powerful imagination can make pictures in your mind to release unhappy experiences and bad feelings. There is a part of your mind that is hidden away called the subconscious. Your subconscious mind does not know the difference between real and pretend. Sometimes you can trick it by making a picture in your mind of the feeling going away.

Make up a story of how you want to release an uncomfortable feeling. Make yourself the hero or heroine of a story. If you like, turn yourself into a superhero. Which superhero would you choose to be? Where would you like to send that feeling? Would you like it to go to the center of the earth or the North Pole? See the feelings coming out of you and rushing off to that safe place. What is the farthest place that you could send your uncomfortable feelings: to the dumpster, the moon, bottom of the ocean, that galaxy far, far away? See yourself banishing your bad feelings. Be tough as you tell them to leave and not come back. See your feeling going through the air to that far away place. Bury them there so they can't return.

<u>Helper Words</u>
I see myself as the hero or heroine in my own story.
I am my own superhero casting out bad feelings.
I send my uncomfortable feelings far, far away.

<u>Tips for parents and teachers</u>: Our unconscious mind cannot tell the difference between what is real and what is imagined. It takes everything literally. Having a sense of control over events by doing a visualization exercise reduces the influence of emotions. This is true even if the sense of control is an illusion. Demonstrate Pull Outs by pantomiming pulling out an upset feeling with your hands and throwing it away.

"I am willing to bring bad feelings to the light
of day and expose them for what they are.

Negative feelings result from false
assumptions and errors in thinking.

They carry uncomfortable body tension
patterns.

They have information for me.

They are something waiting to be worked
out.

Feelings! Bring 'em on. I'll deal with them!

They are only feelings after all."

Lynne Namka   angriesout.com

CHANGING THE COLORS INSIDE YOUR MIND

<u>Objective:</u> To release the dark colors in the visual field associated with unhappy emotions.

<u>Activity:</u> Finding Happy Colors in your Mind. People who can quiet their minds can learn to calm their emotions. You can learn to become quiet inside by closing your eyes and noticing what color you see. If your mind is troubled, you might see gray or dark colors. Breathe deeply into the dark color and keep at it until something changes. Your breath puts oxygen into your body and your brain to calm it down. As you breathe, a brighter, lighter color may come in. Let's take ten long, slow deep breaths and see how the colors in your mind change.

Can you see a light spot or a sliver of another color? Smile at the lighter color and breathe into it and watch it grow larger. Smile and think of something happy and the brighter color will grow. Keep breathing and look for blue, green, purple and yellow and notice how your mood has become lighter. Now try smiling and notice what happens to your mood and the colors you see inside your mind. What colors did you see?

<u>Activity:</u> The Laughing Thymus Thump. Thump your fist over your Thymus (upper middle chest on the left) while smiling and saying "Ha, ha, ha." Exhale, in a rhythm that matches the thumping. Take a deep breath and see how you feel now. Look around, smile and nod at each other or give the "thumbs up" sign. The shortest distance between two people is a smile. The world would be a happier place if we smile at each other. Find someone who might need a special smile today. Smiles are free but they mean a million to someone who needs one. Perhaps that one is yourself.

Sometimes you can trick a bad mood into changing. Smiling can make your mood more positive; turning the corner of the mouth up can actually make you feel better even if it is just for a moment. Controlling your facial expressions, deep breathing and talking with a slower, calm voice can cool the body and emotions down internally. Here are some ideas about smiling:

- One smile can start a friendship.
- Smiles lighten up the room and make others feel friendlier.
- Mistakes can be smiled at and then cleaned up.
- A smile is the most important thing that you wear.
- Smiling is easier. It takes 26 muscles to smile, and 62 muscles to frown.
- Smiling is contagious. Catch a smile from someone and pass it on.
- People who smile a lot are happier than other people.

<u>Activity:</u> Catch a Smile and Pass It On. Let's play Smile Contagion Tag. Think of someone who needs an extra smile today and send them one. Smile, you're it! Pass it on. Smile at everyone, not just your friends. Never run out of smiles and laughter. Now notice how you feel. Happier?

<u>Helper Words:</u>
I'll smile and act happy. Happy is as happy does.
I'll pretend I am happy and hum a happy song.
Thinking of things I'm grateful for can make me smile.
Happy is as happy does. Just Do It!

QUITE 'FRANK'LY...

Smiling, taking a deep breath and tapping on your heart will make you feel much better!

66

ANALYZE YOUR ERRORS TO BECOME THE BEST YOU CAN BE

Objective: To redefine failure as an opportunity to analyze the mistake.

Dialogue: It is okay to make mistakes. Failure is a necessary part of the learning process. Thomas Edison who invented the light bulb said, "I haven't failed. I've identified 10,000 ways this doesn't work." This is called Trial and Error Learning—you try and it doesn't work so you figure out your error and try again. Eventually you get it right and learn heaps of stuff in the process.

Activity: Analyzing and Learning from Errors. Confidence is being able to fail and bounce back. One of the greatest basketball players of all times, Michael Jordan said, "I've missed more than 9000 shots in my career. I've lost almost 300 games. Twenty-six times, I've been trusted to take the game winning shot and I missed. I've failed over and over again in my life. And that is why I succeed." Watch this You Tube video about Michael Jordan and see what ideas you can pick up from him about being the best at what he does.

http://www.mentormob.com/learn/i/positive-messages-growth-mindsets/youtube-michael-jordan-responds-to-lebron-original-video-mashup-maybe-you-should-rise

How do you think Michael Jordan kept on going when he failed so many times when he shot baskets? What inner strength did he have that kept him going? What made Michael Jordan a success when he missed so many shots? Great athletes don't become defensive when they make a mistake and are given criticism. They don't get into the Blame Game. They welcome feedback so they can do better next time. They make videos of themselves so to examine what went wrong. They ask themselves, "How can I correct this? How can I do this better?" They analyze their errors to improve their performance.

Watch if you become defensive when someone criticizes you. Give yourself a break and own your goof up. Tell yourself, "I'll do better next time." Learn from your mistakes and you will become better at what you do. Learn to take feedback about what you did. Figure out what you did wrong so you don't make that mistake again. That is called failing successfully! Then you can feel proud. End the blame game and set yourself free. Once you learn from a mistake it is no longer a mistake. It is a learning opportunity! To improve, watch yourselves fail, and learn from your mistakes. Turn feelings of frustration when criticized into a "Feel Good Moment."

Teacher Cues:
Let's figure out what you did wrong so you can get it right next time.
I fail a lot, so I can help you with that.
You use your smart brain when you discover your mistakes and how to clean them up.
It's good that you use your mind to figure out how to do it right next time.

Helper Words:
I ask myself, "What went wrong? How can I do better?"
I take risks and am confident even if I don't get every single thing right.
I can fail successfully. Confidence is risking and trying and learning from mistakes.
Failure is not fatal. Not trying or giving up is worse than failing and learning.

Never a failure.
Only a lesson.
You are supposed to
makes mistakes.
That's why pencils
have erasers.
Making a mistake and
learning from it is called
growth!

©dianne j. hook

ERROR CORRECTION AND DEALING WITH CRITICISM

<u>Objective</u>: To stop pushing humiliation and shame down and take responsibility for mistakes.

<u>Dialogue</u>: Some people can't stand their uncomfortable feelings of embarrassment and shame when they are criticized. They push them down and turn the blame on someone else. When they are scolded they make excuses or say "It's not my fault." They look for someone else to blame or get angry when scolded and try to block their bad feelings of guilt. They might even blow up to make the other person to back off. Stop and think; did you ever get angry when someone corrected you and said that you were wrong? Getting angry when you are corrected or scolded is a habit you've learned so you won't feel bad inside. You can break this bad habit and learn to deal with your uncomfortable feelings. Get comfortable with your uncomfortable feelings!

One of the biggest lessons in life is to take responsibility. You know what is right and wrong. You are responsible for the things you say and do. You will make some mistakes along the way. Error correction is making things right again. Error correction means cleaning up what you did wrong: It means picking up the living room after you messed it up, saying "I'm sorry" when you hurt someone or replacing something you broke. There are no mistakes when you learn. The only mistake is not trying or giving up. Taking ownership makes you feel proud.

Criticism can be hard to listen to because you feel uncomfortable inside but you might learn something that will help you. Think about a time when you messed up and wanted to hide it. Remember those bad feelings inside when your mom or dad found out what you did? Did you get mad and deny you did it? Think of how proud you could be if you learned from your mistake instead of getting mad. Getting angry or feeling frustrated with yourself when being given feedback makes your problem worse. It can blow up into a big bubble like bubble gum that goes splat in your face!

<u>Activity</u>: No one likes to be told that they did something wrong, but with practice you can learn to handle it. You are supposed to make mistakes. Everyone goofs up from time to time. Let's practice it and move some feelings around. Think of something you did that you got scolded for. Remember you know that you did it and now your got caught. Let's role play some different ways you could react. (Have a child take something from your desk and put it in the trash, then you correct him.)

Acknowledge that it is okay (i.e., human) to have feelings about messing up. Feeling uncomfortable inside may not feel good, but that's not the point. There's no need to do anything else about your internal distress. You don't have to run from bad feelings. Just acknowledge them and breathe into accepting them. Feelings of embarrassment and shame won't hold heavy power over you when you merely accept them for what they are—part of being human.

<u>Helper Words for Children</u>
I can feel good about owning up to my mistakes and accepting the consequences.
It takes courage for me to admit what I did wrong but I take ownership.
I can be kind to myself when I mess up. Live and learn!
Yes! Lesson learned! I can feel proud about learning something about myself.

<u>Tips for parents and teachers</u>: Children by the age of four are beginning moral development and have a sense of what is right and wrong. At this age, you can teach personal responsibility and expect accountability. If you use Time Out as a learning experience (Go think about what happened and how you could handle it differently. Then come and tell me and we can both feel happy) instead of making it a punishment, your children will take more personal responsibility.

Go Past Denial and Defensiveness and Learn from Your Mistakes

What Do You Say When You Are Corrected?

"I didn't do it." Act defensive and put out at the person who corrects you.

"I didn't do it." Become loud and argumentative. How did that feel? If it felt familiar, then you have a problem!

"I did it and I'm sorry!" Yelling that you are sorry because you got caught is getting angry, not true regret. Try again by dropping down into your heart and letting the anger go that you were caught.

I didn't do it." Saying with your head down and feeling guilty and ashamed.

"Okay, it looks like I did it." Say it with an embarrassed, don't want to admit it voice.

"I did it." There, was that so hard to admit? Notice feeling bad inside and staying with uncomfortable feelings. Do you feel regret? Regret is a good feeling to have to help you learn.

"I did it and it was wrong." Take a breath and decide to be responsible. Pat yourself on the back for owning up.

"I did it and it was a mistake I can learn from and feel proud.

"I did it and I'm sorry." Check in with your conscience to see what it has to say. Really feeling sorry for what you did and deciding not to do it any more is growth.

You can 'fess up and feel good about yourself for being honest!

Clip art © www.djinkers.com

TAKE RESPONSIBILITY AND FEEL GOOD ABOUT YOURSELF

<u>Objective:</u> To learn to hear criticism so that mistakes can be corrected.

<u>Dialogue:</u> One of our greatest fears is being caught about being wrong about something. So we learn to become defensive and act as if we didn't do what we are being corrected for. Becoming defensive is not taking responsibility for your own words and actions and turning the blame back on someone else. (Model being defensive and denying that you did something wrong.) Blaming someone else when things go wrong takes away your power to grow and change. This is called the Blame Game. It is a dreadful game because you don't address the problem or learn from an error.

You become a powerful person when you learn to deal with uncomfortable feelings inside when someone criticizes you. Although it may feel uncomfortable, admitting you are wrong can suddenly make things right again. It clears the air. You are strong and resilient when you learn to handle criticism that might help you. Accepting responsibility for what you did wrong allows you to take charge of your life. If you lose your cool, you give up your control. Another person's actions may make it harder for you to keep your temper, but the responsibility is all yours.

<u>Activity:</u> End the Blame Game. People blame others because they want to get away from the bad feelings inside themselves. You will be happier when you are responsible for correcting your own mistakes. If you learn something positive about yourself, you didn't make a mistake—it was just part of your learning process. Blame keeps you in the victim mode repeatedly throwing the problem on someone else. Blaming others distracts you away from the real place of power which is within yourself. But you can learn to deal with those bad feelings when criticized.

Why not bypass blame and go directly to taking responsibility for your own well being! Think of a past mistake that you made. Remember, to improve, we can watch ourselves fail, and learn from our mistakes. (Write these words on the board: "It's only a mistake that I can clean up. Yup, I did it. I can own it. I handle any uncomfortable feelings when I'm corrected I'm stronger than the feelings of discomfort inside. I end the Blame Game move on.") Draw a picture of you goofing up and write one of the sentences on it.

<u>Activity:</u> Pretending You are Older or Younger. Pretend you are two years older and more grownup than you are now. Acting more capable and grownup makes you feel better about yourself seeing yourself as more mature. The opposite is true also. When you act younger than your age or act in immature ways, you feel worse about yourself. So free yourself up. Admit your wrongness!

<u>Helper Words</u>
Believing "I can't be wrong" is faulty thinking. I correct this error.
I can be comfortable with my uncomfortable feelings. So what? They are just feelings.
I can hear criticism and feel good about learning from it.
I go past blame and go right to problem solving.

<u>Tips for parents and teachers:</u> Gay Hendrix, author of several books on healthy living, says, "Mental health problems are basically disturbances of responsibility. Neurotics take too much responsibility' people with character disorders take too little. As a human, you tend to see and experience responsibility as a burden or a restriction of your freedom, when, in fact, it is the path to wholeness and to incredible freedom and light. It is exhilarating to know yourself to be wholly responsible for your life." Remind your family members that they are responsible for anger outbursts and they can learn to express anger in ways that do not hurt others or themselves. Taking ownership of what you did and uncomfortable feelings is so healing.

YOU WILL MESS UP. SO WHAT?

Mess happens, right?

Think about how your room
gets messy.

It's up to you what you do about it.

Make a mistake?

YOU KNOW WHAT TO DO!

Clean it up.

BECOME A TAKE-CHARGE PERSON

<u>Objective</u>: To learn to analyze mistakes and become accountable.

<u>Dialogue</u>: Everyone makes mistakes. They are a part of learning. It is what you do after you make a mistake that counts. If you slip up and act in a way you dislike, think what went wrong and how you could have handled it differently Tell yourself that you made an error and can act differently next time by breathing and slowing things down. Being defensive means getting upset when someone gives you feedback. You are not necessarily a bad person if you become defensive. You just haven't learned the skill of handling feedback and criticism. Defensiveness is a way of acting that you do without thinking. You can just a good person having a bad habit of acting defensive to avoid taking responsibility.

A common myth is that you have no control over your feelings. You and only you are responsible for your thinking and the way you think creates the type of life that you will create. No one else can get inside your head and push that button marked anger. Nobody but you has the power to pull your chain or your pull your trigger. Only you make yourself feel what you feel. The bottom line is that you are always responsible for what you think, say and do. Taking responsibility for your own actions makes you feel better about yourself.

<u>Activity</u>: Respecting Yourself. When the old way of doing things doesn't work for you, learn something new. Being responsible means that you are accountable in your words and deeds. Being reliable and taking responsibility for words and actions is a sign of maturity. Accept your share of the responsibility for what happened if you want to feel good about yourself. Take ownership with the slogan of "Make a mess and clean it up!" Own your goof up and take a deep breath to clear your mind about what to do. "Sometimes you actually want to make them. Let's practice making a mistake and not getting upset. Write your name and spell it wrong. Laugh and say, "Oops I can fix that."

Tell yourself, "Mistakes are part of my learning. They are proof that I'm trying." Mistakes happen. It is what I do with it that counts." Of course it is better to make new mistakes and not keep repeating the same old ones. The first step in releasing guilt about goofing up is to remind yourself about what your part of the problem was. Clean it up by acknowledging what you did wrong and then stop doing it! Respect for yourself comes when you own your part of the problem and clean it up.

<u>Helper Words:</u>
I make a pact with myself to be responsible for what I say and do.
I stop believing that other people are responsible for making me angry.
I'm in charge here. I can talk about this conflict and work it out.
It's is okay for me to feel this uncomfortable feeling. I can learn something here.

<u>Tips for parents and teachers</u>: Children who have a fear of being criticized cannot handle the negative emotions that surface when being corrected so the child stops listening to reasonable criticisms or requests. The defensive child can become agitated and angry when adults set reasonable limits or ground him for misbehavior. When you are correcting your child say, "You can handle hearing this criticism. "Breathe into uncomfortable feelings and tell yourself, "I am strong and I need to hear this." Use affirmation cues such as, "I'm proud of you for owning up to what you did. I know you will make a better choice next time. Smile and feel good about yourself. I'm proud of you for being a caring person. You're one fantastic kid for _____." Use the questions and ideas presented in the Cool Dude worksheet after putting your child in Time Out a learning experience.

Do you have good friends?

Are you a good friend to others?

Is your relationship balanced?

You set the rules of what you will stand for from others.

You teach people how to treat you through setting boundaries or not setting them!

Respect yourself and people will respect you!

Lynne Namka   nardar.com   HappyHealthyLoving.com

TAP, LOVE AND BREATHE

<u>Objective:</u> To learn breathing and self-acupressure to break into giving up on a hard task.

<u>Dialogue:</u> Do you have a bad habit of getting upset with yourself when you are discouraged? Do you go into the Blame Game and beat yourself up for making a mistake? Negative self talk is the bad things that others have told you what you are when they were in a bad mood. You don't have to take on negative labels from others. (Write TLC and TLB on the board. Underneath write Tender Loving Care and Tap, Love and Breathe.)

TLB stands for Tap, Love and Breathe or tender loving behavior. It is a form of TLC which is Tender Loving Care which you can do when you need an attitude adjustment. You have a choice about staying stuck in your bad feeling or using a feeling-moving tool to change it. You can learn tools to release your bad feelings. Tap, Love and Breathe takes you out of stuck feelings. Your breath is a great tool to help put more oxygen in your body and break into an unhappy mood. Your lungs will love you for doing this.

<u>Activity:</u> Get Past Frustration with Tap, Love and Breathe. Think of a bad habit such as getting mad at yourself when you do something wrong. Take a deep breath while you tap and forgive yourself for becoming upset. Say your feeling out loud to hear your own voice: "Even though I get frustrated and want to give up when I have trouble learning something new, I forgive myself and keep on working."

Think about that painful habit of getting frustrated and discouraged. Would you like to let it go? Have you ever gone across the monkey bars? Picture moving from bar to bar in your mind. What do you have to do to get to the next rung? C. S. Lewis who wrote *The Chronicles of Narnia* said, "Getting over a painful experience is much like crossing the monkey bars. You have to let go at some point in order to move on." Cup your fingers and tap briskly all over your body starting from the head down to your toes while you breathe deeply. Tap up and down on the front and back of your arms and legs. Tap on as much of your neck and back as you can reach. Repeat these letting go statements.

I Am Willing:
I am willing to let go of my feeling about _____.
I am willing to stop being irritable and grouchy.
I am willing to breathe and tap to calm my mind.

I Choose:
I choose to release the feelings of _____ in my mind.
I choose to release all frustration about _____from my body.
I choose to make better decisions on how I act.

I Accept:
I accept myself even if I get upset about _____.
I accept all my emotions, even my frustrated and unhappy ones.
I accept I am a real human being who sometimes has bad feelings.

Stressed? Ohm it out!

Lynne Namka *HappyHealthyLiving.com*

Ohm is the universal sound for calming.
See yourself becoming how you want to be.
Cool yourself off by deep breathing.
Talk yourself down when you are upset.
Be willing to be the Change Maker.

Become Your Own Captain of Change!

AVOID ZOMBIE THOUGHTS THAT SEND YOU DOWN THAT DANGER ROAD

Objective: To recognize that feeling bad about yourself or feeling bored can result in making a poor decision.

Dialogue: Everyone wants to be happy. Is that right? Happiness is not about owning things or doing risky things that might cause harm to you or others. When we feel good about ourselves, it's easy to make good decisions. But sometimes when we feel bad about ourselves, we give ourselves permission to make poor choices. We can take on wrong ideas from other people who are negative and don't feel good about themselves. Not good!

Your words have power over your mood. Poor decisions start with Zombie Thoughts who try to suck the life out of you. Zombie Thoughts leave you zapped and grey and lifeless. When you get down or feel sorry for yourself, Zombie Thoughts try to convince you to do risky things. They say that it doesn't matter if you do things you know are harmful.

Activity: Understanding Zombie Thoughts. If you feel discouraged and stop caring about yourself, watch out. Your mood has gone into a downward spiral of feeling bad, then worse, and then REALLY bad. That's when Zombie thoughts come in to tempt you down that Danger Road. What do you say to put yourself down? Why do you think good kids sometimes make poor choices? Describe some poor decisions. I'll list them on the board.

Beating yourself up with ugly words.
Not caring about your school work and giving up
Giving up on yourself leaving you open to poor influences.
Acting out in harmful ways when you are angry.
Telling yourself that you don't care and taking dumb risks.
Feeling sorry for yourself.
Doing things you know are wrong.

Why Good Kids Might Make Poor Choices:
You feel discouraged because the grownups in your life let you down.
You've been beating yourself with words like "I'm worthless, I'm no good, I'm dumb," etc.
You've been telling yourself that no one cares so it doesn't matter what you do.
You try to get away from your own problems and distract yourself from feeling bad.
You feel like you don't belong and seek out the kids who do risky things.
You are bored and seek excitement.
You are trying to relieve stress and think something risky is cool.
You want to act like the older kids and grow up faster.

Zombie thoughts are dangerous to your self-esteem. It all comes back to what you put your mind on. What you think about determines the quality and direction of your life. Bad thoughts and a bad attitude are things that you have a choice over. Watch out that you don't just drift into things that are harmful for you because it is easy. Going along with alcohol, drugs or gangs when you are down on yourself might send you down that Danger Road. There are times in your life when you just have to walk away from things that you know aren't good for you.

ZOMBIE THOUGHTS SUCK THE LIFE OUT OF YOU LEAVING YOU GREY AND LIFELESS.

They tell you to beat yourself up with ugly words, make poor choices,
act out in harmful ways when you are angry, take dumb risks and do unsafe things.
Nothing harms you as much as Zombie thoughts living inside your head.

I STOP SAYING UGLY WORDS ABOUT MYSELF.

I STOP ALL MEAN WORDS THAT CREATE SELF-HATRED.

PUNCTURING THOSE ZOMBIE THOUGHTS

<u>Objective:</u> To deflate thoughts that create self-hatred.

<u>Dialogue:</u> Sometimes you know what you are doing just isn't working for you. Zombie Thoughts are full of self-hatred. They can't be escaped from running from them. They get worse if you run to poor choices like smoking, doing drugs, alcohol and other risky activities that might feel good temporarily, but make you feel even worse about yourself. They cause you to lose your Mojo. So when you've been down in the dumps because you've been hard on yourself, look for your Mojo deep inside yourself.

Don't kick yourself in the self-esteem when you are down. Go towards the things that will boost your self-esteem by living your positive values and signature strengths. Don't let others talk you out of or make fun of the good things you stand for. Don't be afraid to say no to trouble and yes to yourself. You are an expert on yourself. You know what is best for you.

<u>Activity:</u> Stick that Zombie Thought with a Pin. Close your eyes and visualize a Zombie Thought of "I'm no good, stupid, dumb, ugly, fat, etc," and see it trying to harm you. Turn around and face the Zombie Thoughts. They are just your fears that are full of hot air. Visualize a gigantic pin with a sharp point. Picture yourself with a superhero look on your face sticking the Zombie Thoughts so that it deflates and zips away in the air like a punctured balloon. Give it some sound effects— Whoosh!

Know what your own particular Danger Road looks like and how you will end up if you choose it. See yourself saying no to a risky activity and feeling good. Saying no wisely to harmful things can be the best thing that you do for yourself.

If ever you hear yourself say, "Things are so hard for me that I'm no good so I'll just give up." Stop and give yourself a good talking to. If you start to think that you are unlovable or unworthy, tell yourself "Whoa. Don't go there. Just don't go there." Don't tolerate disrespect, especially not from yourself.

<u>Tips for parents and teachers:</u> The temptation in young people for exciting activities can be stronger than adults realize. Attraction to risky actions is related to greater activity in the orbitofrontal cortex, an area of the brain related to rewards and the inferior frontal gyrus, an area for self-control. People have a limited amount of self-control that dwindles when used to cope with stress, temptation and other challenges to will power. When we feel bad, we are more vulnerable to impulsive, undesirable behavior. Self-control can fail when the strength of an impulse and the need for reward exceeds the capacity to regulate it. We can teach children cognitive control of their thoughts to help them resist temptations.

"Happiness starts from the inside out.

Being in a happy place
is an inside job.

It starts with your thoughts.

You can choose the quality
of your thoughts.

Interrupt the negative,
put in the positive.

Think happy. Act happy.

Off you go now to
your happy place.

Lynne Namka   **HappyHealthyLoving.com**

DON'T BULLY YOURSELF WITH MEAN THOUGHTS

<u>Objective:</u> To stop self blame and derogatory thoughts.

<u>Dialogue:</u> Sometimes we say mean things about ourselves. Bully words or negative self talk come from the bad things that others have said about us when they were in a bad mood. Sometimes we believe those ugly words. We get into a bad habit of thinking bad thoughts secretly or saying them about ourselves out loud. When we are down, we get into a bad habit of beating ourselves up with hateful bully words. You might have the mistaken idea that you are unlovable or that you don't deserve respect. This is inaccurate information based on some false beliefs that you picked up when you were younger. You might believe that you don't have rights or that your needs don't matter. If someone says bad things about you such as "You are stupid" or "You are dumb," don't believe their lies. Hateful words that you've heard from others about yourself aren't true. Don't repeat them to yourself. Don't believe them. You're too smart to believe the ugly words of others.

<u>Activity:</u> Get Tough with a Firm Gesture. Thought Stoppage is interrupting the unwanted idea in your mind and sending it packing. Sometimes you might say mean things to yourself as if you have a bully inside your mind. Give me some ideas like "I am stupid, I hate myself or I'm no good, etc." and I'll write them on the board. Are those helpful or unhelpful thoughts? Are those good messages to have in your mind? What do you want to do with bullying thoughts like these?

(Erase the words lightly while saying, "Stop you ugly thought. Get out of my mind." Use a wet towel to completely erase the words. Let a few volunteers come up to the board to write their negative thoughts privately by covering them with their bodies and then erasing them.)

False ideas that make you reject yourself are like playground bullies. We can either feel bad about them or challenge them. Let's challenge them using your wonderful imagination. Think of a troublesome thought that keeps creeping up on you. Get out your imaginary erasers. Break into a negative by giving yourself a strong command to cut it out. Tell yourself, "I won't give ugly thoughts free rent in my brain!" (Write these Thought Stoppage words on the board.)

Adding a gesture such as shrugging your shoulders or pretending to push the thought away makes it stronger. Think of a second bully thought you don't like. Now brush the thought off your shoulder or shrug it off. Or make a screeching sound and pretend to put on the brakes on the thought. Tell yourself quite firmly, "Stop! Don't go there. Just don't go there," while pushing your hand out in the stop position. Scold that thought by saying, "Don't speak to me like that. Let's practice your doing these Thought Stoppage ideas. Think of a negative idea and say these sentences out loud. (Encourage the children to get loud with their commands by saying, "Louder. I can't hear you!")

Do you do Thought Stoppage already to break into that bully inside your mind? What do you do when an internal idea you don't like bugs you? What do you tell yourself when you're tired of the ugly words taking over your mind? (Write the children's examples of how they take control of their mind on the board.) Remind yourself to break into that bully in your mind saying, "I'm not all that bad. I refuse to think that way." Practice makes permanent when you put in a new habit.

<u>Helper Words</u>
I'm not all that bad. Sometimes I mess up, that's all. Some parts of me are pretty good.
Even though _____ said _____ about me, I refuse to believe it.
I push hateful thoughts away and say I won't go there."

Be Your Own BFF

See how powerful you are.
Write five positive, loving
Things about yourself.

• _____
• _____
• _____
• _____
• _____

Two more things!
You are a marvelous person
with feelings!
Be gentle and loving with yourself.

Love is a language
we all understand.

Clip art © www.djinkers.com

TAKE A HIKE AND WALK AWAY FROM PEOPLE WHO HURT YOU

<u>Objective</u>: To discriminate between friends and those who are not helpful

<u>Dialogue</u>: What is a friend? Everybody isn't your friend just because they let you hang out with them. Some people want to put you down and rain on your parade while pretending that they like you. A friend is someone who likes you and treats you well. Actions speak louder than words so we look at person's actions to see if they are friendly or not. People who need drama sometimes say things that aren't kind.

We have different levels of friends. Think of the center of a bull's eye. (Draw a bull's eye on the board with a heart inside the center circle.) At the center of our circle of friends, we have our true friends. They are the ones who really care about you and you care about them. Your true "Heart Friends" fit in the center of the bull's eye. True friends take time and energy so we usually have only one or two at a time. The next circle out is your "Hang out" Friends or the people you like to do things with. The next circle out is your Activity Friends" or the people you play sports with or are in clubs with but you are not close to. Next is Acquaintances who are people you know and speak to but aren't special to you. If you have one or two really good heart friends, you are lucky.

<u>Activity:</u> Let's find out what true friends are by watching the cartoon *True Friends*. http://www.youtube.com/watch?v=PJDOcr0P8cY by Notebook Babies.

True friends are like big umbrellas; they always have you covered. Know your real friends and don't give yourself away to people who don't deserve your friendship. Sometimes you can be too loyal to people who aren't loyal to you back. You might be trying to hang out with people who don't value you and put you down. You might find yourself playing with people who aren't being kind to you. Sometimes they say mean things or refuse to play with you on some days. With Hot and Cold Friends, one day you are in and the next day you are out. They like big drama!

Some people suck the happiness out of you. Just because they say they have your back, doesn't mean they won't stab you in it. You don't have to stay and put up with it because you want to fit in? If someone makes you feel like you don't fit in, you may feel like you have to give up part of yourself to belong. Never give up your values to fit in. Open your eyes and notice what's going on. Watch which people in your group turn on others to make them feel bad. If you believe in yourself and that you deserve to be treated kindly, you know this type of person can't be a true friend.

You can get fed up with being treated poorly and tell yourself enough is enough and it's time to leave. Fed up is a first cousin to healthy anger. Sometimes it helps to become fed up with being treated bad so you will leave. Being fed up with someone who is being mean to you helps you get the energy and momentum to take a hike. Take action! Action is the solution to feeling bad when you are being treated badly or unjustly by someone. Tell yourself, "I don't have to hang around people who are mean to me. Wow, that's impressive!" Hard times show you who your true friends are. Keep looking for new friends that like you for who you are.

<u>Teacher Cues:</u>
Are you showing that you are a true friend today?
What could you do when you feel threatened by a classmate or sibling?
How do you know if a person is a good friend or not?
Should you give another chance to someone who keeps saying hurtful things to you?

High drama doesn't have legs.

It doesn't walk in by itself.

Stop creating or inviting High Drama.

Stop giving it bystander power.

Stop hanging out with the worst sort of adrenalin junkies.

You do have legs and can walk away!

Lynne Namka   Nardar.com

USE YOUR BREATH TO KEEP YOUR COOL

<u>Objective:</u> To breathe at the first sign of threat.

<u>Dialogue:</u> Most everyone holds their breath when they are scared or stressed. When we were little and got scolded or hit or rejected or didn't know what to say, we tried to make ourselves seem smaller by squeezing the body and holding our breath. We learned to hold our breath to try to squish the feelings in order to keep from feeling bad. Holding your breath when you are scared is a bad habit. Contracting your body in tight and stopping your breath keeps you from getting good oxygen to deal with whatever upsets you. People hold their breath just when they need oxygen the most. Have you ever held your breath for a few seconds when you were scared?

(Demonstrate how your lungs are squeezed together by pulling your shoulders together, putting your head down and holding your breath. Then show the opposite of spreading your arms outward to expand the chest, taking a deep breath and stretching. Have the children experience and exaggerate these two closed and open body reactions. Ask them to describe how it feels to be closed in or open.)

<u>Activity:</u> Be a Cool Dude. Breathe! Just Breathe! Notice how you felt when your breath was shut off by tensing your body and pulling in. Whenever you are scared or angry, use your breath to make yourself strong and powerful! Your breath is your best friend! It will always be with you when you need to calm yourself down. Your lungs will be happy as you release the wastes of carbon dioxide from your body. Out with old stale air. In with new fresh air.

(Hold your hands out and move then in and out like an accordion.) Pretend that your lungs are like an accordion. Move your hands with me and notice your breathing going in and out. Take big breaths to make them open and close wide. Make your breath go down deep into your body as far as you can. Deep breathing which goes down past your ribs into the belly helps you relax. Cool Dude's know how to calm themselves with their breath. Let's try three different types of breaths.

1. Take a long, slow breath and count to see how long you can hold your breath. Take a deep breath and hold it. (Count out loud slowly to ten.) Now exhale slowly while I count and blow your breath completely out. Blow all your stress and bad feelings out. Make your belly soft.

2. Next let's do the half breaths. Take a half breath in and hold. Take a full breath in and hold. Now exhale half way and hold. Then exhale your breath out fully. Blow out unhappy and fearful thoughts.

3. A third type of breath is fast as you go up a musical scale in your mind with the tune Do, Re, Me, Fa, La, So, Te, Do. Breathe quickly like you are going up musical steps up, up, up, up seven times and then go down the steps with the fast breaths.

To be a Cool Dude, breathe! Just breathe! Which type of breathing did you like? Do all three types when you feel upset and shut your breath down. Mix it up!

<u>Helper Words for Children</u>
I take a deep breath and when I don't know what to do.
I make my breath go deeper and deeper down in my body.
I take deep breaths to calm myself down.
Just breathe. I tell myself, just breathe.

Your breath is your best friend and it's always with you!

Tune into your breathing. Take charge of putting life-giving oxygen into your body.

Pump up your energy by taking the three breaths.

1. The Long,Long, Long Deep breath.
2. The Two Ups and Two Downs Breaths.
3. The 7-Up and the 7-Down The Musical Scale Breaths.

For even more energy, tap on your head and body and smile!

©dianne j. hook

SOOTHE YOURSELF WITH MINDFULNESS BREATHING

<u>Objective:</u> To push the breath deep into the diaphragm to create more oxygen in the body.

<u>Dialogue:</u> Did you ever think, "I'm so stressed out. I can't deal with this?" Negative thoughts that scare you are a sign that your mind is trying to trick you. Don't let "I'm so stressed. I'm so overwhelmed." Challenge your unruly mind when it tries to convince you that you can't handle something. Tell yourself, "Stress you are not the boss of me!" There are many ways to use your breath to calm yourself. Let's watch this cartoon video from You Tube called 4-7-8 Breathing Exercise by GoZen http://www.youtube.com/watch?v=Uxbdx-SeOOo.

<u>Activity:</u> Mindfulness Breathing. Mindfulness is just observing rather than reacting to your feelings. You watch instead of getting upset. Watch what you say to stress yourself out. Let's sit quietly and breathe deep into your belly and learn about your body tension patterns.

> Be aware of your body when you become upset.
> Watch what happens in your body when you feel stressed.
> Tension patterns come and go. Just watch them.
> Just watch how the body reacts to stress.
> Watch your stomach as it gets nervous.
> Watch the tension in your neck, and your jaw.
> Watch how you hold your breath.
> Breathe into the tightness.
> Tell the part of your body that gets tight to relax.
> Use your breath to relax the tight places in your body.
> Mindfully watch. Don't judge. Just stay present and watch.
> It's just a tight place that wants some breath.
> Use your friendly breath to break into tension and stress.
> Breath rising. Breath falling.
> Breathing in. Breathing out.
> Soft belly. Make your belly soft.
> Taking in. Giving out.
> In. Out.

Where did you feel tension? Could you breathe it out of your body? It only takes one person to change your life—YOU! You can be the changer when you don't like the negativity going on in your mind. Don't let your negative mind shoot you down. In order to change, you must change how your mind thinks while fueling your body with deep belly breaths.

<u>Helper Words</u>
I keep my attitude clean and bright.
I believe in my ability to breathe and change my attitude.
The worst thing I can do is give in to a bad attitude.
No negativity for me. I blow out unhappy thoughts.

<u>Tips for parents and teachers:</u> When you notice a child is anxious or angry, send him or her to You Tube to watch this video about self-soothing again. Ask them to find what unhelpful things they were saying that was so upsetting and identify some Helper Words to replace them.

Stressed? Stuck?

Write out the options.
Drop into your heart.
Breathe into the place
where fear resides.
You are more powerful
than your fear beliefs.
There's something inside you
that's greater than any belief
that keeps you stuck.

Your Wisdom Box
has the answers
you need.

©dianne j. hook

SOMETIMES YOU SAY YES, SOMETIMES YOU SAY NO

<u>Objectives:</u> To feel good about being assertive and saying "No" when appropriate.

<u>Dialogue:</u> Are you the kind of person who has trouble saying no to people? For many of us it's hard to say no when others ask us for favors or when we have something we think we 'have' to do something that they want to fit in with the group. And so what ends up happening? When you don't want to do something, do you agree to because you are afraid of hurting someone else's' feelings? Some people do things that are harmful to them because they are afraid to say what they think.

You have a "Wisdom Box" within you that knows right from wrong. Some people call this your intuition or your conscience. Imagine if you had a wise place inside you where you could go and get answers. Your common sense and Wisdom Box can work together to help you figure things out when you get confused. Sometimes you feel confused because some information is missing and you may need to ask some questions. If you breathe deeply and become really quiet and listen inside, sometimes you can get answers. How do you know what is right or wrong for you to do?

<u>Activity:</u> Write these ways to say no and several Yeses on slips of paper for the children to choose.

That doesn't fit for me.	Uh huh, not for me.	No, not right now.
I don't want to.	No. Thank you.	No! I said no!

Here's some questions which will give you practice checking in with your Wisdom Box: Do you want some woozles? Will you help me cheat on this test? Do you want some green eggs and ham? Let's be mean to ___. Show me your answers on the test. Want some ice cream? Let's go hurt someone. I'd like to give you a snack, okay? A smack? How about a whack? Hey take this pill to feel good. Do you want more knocks on the head? Let's mess up the room. Give me all your money. Will you eat this yucky food? I can disrespect you, right? Yes or no?

Yes means yes, no means no. It can be hard to say no at times because of fear of rejection. Some people are so keen to fit in that they say and do things that compromise their integrity. You don't have to do things you know are wrong. If you want to say no, don't agree to do it. Actions speak louder than words. Walk away from a person who tries to get you to change your mind after you have said no. Remember your courage. They know that keeping you there is a way to wear you down. As long as you stick around, they might talk you into something you don't want. Just get up and walk away. Let your feet say what you mean. Walking away can be the strongest no you can say. You can choose. You can ALWAYS choose.

<u>Teacher Cues:</u>
Say what fits for you. Make yourself proud.
Remember you can always ask for what you want. You may not get it but you can ask.
You can choose. You have the right to choose what is best for you.
"No." is a complete sentence. Respect someone who says no to you.

<u>Helper Words:</u>
I know what is right or wrong. I make myself proud.
I visualize myself slamming a heavy metal garage door down when I say No and mean it.
I can check with my Wisdom Box to get the best answer to know what is absolutely best for me.
I can say what I mean and mean what I say.

WAYS TO DEAL WITH THREAT

Objective: To learn better coping strategies to deal with feeling threatened.

Dialogue: Let's pretend that you are a cave man or woman and a saber tooth tiger jumps out in front of you and growls. Of course you would feel threatened and scared. What might you do when you feel a big threat? (List the five ways that people move when they are threatened or stressed on the board. Have the children draw stick figures to illustrate each response when dealing with an aggressor.)

1. Move toward the threat (fight back and return the negative energy).
2. Move away from the threat (Run away. Sometimes this is an appropriate choice.)
3. Move away from the threat in the mind (feel helpless and space out).
4. Stay present and let the threat hurt you (give in to the aggressor.)
5. Stay present to deal with the problem (stand up to the aggressor, problem solve.)

The first three ways are called the "Fight, flight or freeze" responses. You can give in to the person or you can take a deep breath to clear your mind and address the problem directly. (Discuss these natural responses to threat.)

Activity: Step Back in your Mind when Threatened. Today we don't have saber tooth tigers but sometimes aggressive people threaten or scare us. Think of a time when you felt threatened or bullied. Can anyone give an example of feeling threatened and we'll do a role play about it. (Have the children role play these five ways and ask them how they felt with each response. Set up some scenes of threat such as someone calls you an ugly name or grabs your paper.)

Knowing positive actions to take when you are threatened makes you feel more powerful! Your breath is your best friend and it is always there with you. You can call up your deep breath which brings oxygen to your cells to give you energy. Breathing calms your mind when you are scared or confused. Breathing helps calm the fight, flight or freeze reaction so that you can stay present and deal with the situation. Deep breathing helps think more clearly!

Sometimes you can tell the person what they are doing that you don't like. Other times it's not safe to share your feelings. When should you should walk away and not tell the other person why you are leaving?" (Most children can discriminate situations when it would be dangerous to express their anger.) When things are at their worst, promise me you will believe in your ability to find people who treat you well. Hang out with people who will treat you well and be a good friend back.

Helper Words:
I can let go of what I don't need.
I make good choices when I feel threatened.
I take a deep breath and decide do I need to negotiate or leave?
I am the Change Maker! I am the Captain of Change!"

Tips for parents and teachers: Ask your children about whether they are being bullied occasionally reminding them that verbal harassment is a type of bullying. Most children do not share these experiences with adults on a regular basis. Remind them of the different ways they can cope with threat. Ask them what they do to calm themselves down. Compliment your children when they do self-soothing techniques on their own. Be sparing of your praise and it will be worth something.

"You have a step-back circuit in your brain that brakes and inhibits responses.

It's there but you have to activate it by stepping back and taking a breath before you act.

**Triggered?
It's think, before reacting time;
not react before thinking.**

Take that step-back, make-a-better-choice moment."

Lynne Namka   angriesout.com

THE POWER POSE CAN SHIFT THE DOUBTING MIND

<u>Objective:</u> To experience standing tall and using body postures of strength.

<u>Dialogue:</u> How you act determines how you feel. The Act As If theory says that your actions guide your emotions (laugh and you will feel happy). If you want to have a trait, act as if you already have it. Taking a pose of power actually makes you feel better about yourself. Have you ever seen a cat or dog puff up to look bigger than they are so they will be taken seriously?

<u>Activity:</u> Let's practice some power poses. Check your mood first on a scale of one to ten. Think of a time when you won or accomplished something really great and raise your arms in a V-shape and lift your chin up. This is the "Yes! I've done it" power position which increases endorphins and makes you feel good. Take your power by making your body as big as possible by raising your arms and stretching them out wide. Pull your body up and pull your arms back to open up your lungs and ribs to give you more oxygen. Leaning back in a chair with your arms behind your head and your feet up is a power pose. Check your mood again.

Low power poses where you give up your power are slouching, pulling yourself in to seem invisible, holding your neck and making yourself small. Any pose with your head down that squeezes your lungs inward will make you look insignificant to others and they dismiss you as not being important. Beliefs and hunched over body language like "I'm not worthy, I'm not safe," and ""I don't belong here," convey a message that you don't believe in yourself. And it sends a message to your own brain as well.

Body posture changes can change your mind and your mind can change your behavior. Standing tall and acting powerful can change how you think about yourself. There is a saying, "Fake it until you make it," and that holds truth. Stop making yourself small and unimportant. Do the Power Poses for one minute a day. Sit tall and think "I can do this, I'm strong enough." Smile while visualizing yourself as positive and self-assured. Thoughts become action, and then action becomes thoughts.

<u>Activity:</u> Let's do some power poses for one minute to build a new sense of presence about yourself. Which pose do you like? Fill your lungs with air and expand your body. Upgrade your body by making yourself bigger to display strength, power and pride. Act as if you are confident. Do it until you become it! Pretend to be confident while you do the power poses. Let your body fake out your mind. Fake it until you become it! It is really the true you. The head down is the false you.

Practice the body language of confidence even when you don't feel sure of yourself and your body will create the hormone of testosterone and your stress hormones will go down. Get comfortable with allowing your light to shine while projecting a position of "I'm strong and confident." Imprint this message on your mind while expanding your body will boost your morale. Get comfortable with the Power Poses and give a message of confidence and certainty to the world. Teach this posture to your younger brothers and sisters.

<u>Activity:</u> For older children, watch part of psychologist Amy Cuddy's video on You Tube: Your body language shapes who you are at http://www.youtube.com/watch?v=Ks-_Mh1QhMc

Ten Things Happy People Do!

Practice loving kindness.

Make good and loyal friends.

Keep a positive outlook.

Enjoy the little things in life.

Commit to goals and get them done.

Correct mistakes instead of blaming others.

Stand and walk tall showing confidence.

Have a giving heart and help others.

Express gratitude.

Forgive themselves and others.

Clip art © www.djinkers.com

BYSTANDER POWER AND BCOMING A HERO

<u>Objective:</u> To learn to step up and speak out against bullying.

<u>Dialogue:</u> What is bully behavior? Bullies play up to an audience and feed on group approval. They try to get others to laugh at the victim. If one person stands up to a bully, then others can join in. There is strength and safety in numbers—that is Bystander Power! Bystander Power works because people who bully don't like to face a crowd that disapproves of their behavior. That's right—when one person speaks up when bullying is going on and says that it is wrong, then others can speak up too. If more people stood up to bullies, we'd have less bullying!

Doing nothing or laughing when a classmate is bullied encourages bullying behavior. Standing by and ignoring what is going on gives the bully permission to keep hurting their victim. Bullies love an audience and they like to have support from others. Humiliating a victim in the presence of others gives them more enjoyment. Your being silent encourages inappropriate behavior. Bullies feel good when you laugh at the mean things they say and do. What do you think about someone who feels pleasure when they see another person suffer misfortune? People with low self-esteem are more likely to bully with the mistaken idea that they elevate their position by picking on someone else.

What does it means to be a bully helper or assistant? Have you ever helped someone else be a bully? You could be a hero instead. Don't wait for someone else to step up and stop bullying. Be an everyday hero and say "Hey, that's not fair. Stop that." If you can't confront the bully directly, step forward and tell the victim "Let's go. Let's get out of here."

Chances are there are many things in your life that you would like to do but you are afraid of. Fear stops you. Build a strong habit of becoming courageous and walking through what frightens you. Stare down those things that intimidate you. The more you challenge your fear, the more courage you will have. Developing courage gives you control over your life. It makes you into a hero.

<u>Activity:</u> Bullied Girl Voted the Ugliest on the Internet Gives an AMAZING Speech. Listen to how this girl got past how she looks and what she had to say about dealing with internet bullying. Have you ever been teased because of how you looked? Each one of us has a message to give to our world. What would you say to her? Tell of a time when you reached out to someone who was hurting. http://www.youtube.com/watch?v=R0OV92Yyl20

<u>Teacher Cues:</u> Become a Bully Buster!
If you laugh when someone is being hurt, you give power to the bully.
Don't give approval by laughing at someone who does cruel things to others.
Take a stand. Don't let another kid's right to be safe be taken away.
Do not feed the local bullies! Be courageous and take your power.

<u>Helper Words:</u>
Hey, no nasty words here. That's not right. Leave him alone!"
I'll be a hero and speak up against people being disrespected.
I disagree with mean remarks. I say "That's not funny, man. Cut it out!"
If he says it's a joke say, "That's not funny."

Take your Bystander Power

Stand tall and speak up.

Tune into the wise thing to do.

Step up and act with courage.

Ask your friends to join you.

Be brave and state what you stand for.

Stand firm and say,

"We treat people fairly."

Clip art © www.djinkers.com

FINDING YOUR COURAGE

<u>Objective:</u> To learn to deal with uncomfortable feelings when faced with a moral dilemma.

<u>Dialogue:</u> Think about a time when you had to stick up for yourself or someone else. It might be scary to do something that others might disapprove of. Yet sometimes you have to find that strong place within yourself and do the right thing. Can anyone tell us about taking a stand that you were uncertain of? Was there another time that you didn't speak up because you were afraid? Sometimes we don't speak out because there would be bad consequences if we did. Sometimes the best thing to do is stay quiet so that someone won't get hurt.

Other times we hold back because we are feeling uneasy and uncomfortable inside. A big fear is fear of feelings. Avoidance of uncomfortable feelings because you are afraid of them is an irrational fear that can be challenged. Scary feelings can be felt, given a name and accepted.

<u>Activity:</u> Find your Courage to Say, "That's Not Fair. Cut it Out!" You and your friends can stand together to speak up against bullying and unfair behavior. Someone has to be the first to speak out and call bullying for what it is. You can tip the scales and interrupt bullying. It takes courage. Give me examples of what courage is. Courage is doing that which you fear and standing up for what you believe. Have you ever spoken out even though you were afraid to help someone out? Don't tolerate mean behavior. Believe that you can speak out and you are half way there. Then make yourself proud by speaking up. (Ask the children to comment on this quote from Missy Good.)

"Courage, her mother had once told her, was not simply the fact that you weren't scared of anything… it was being scared and doing whatever it was anyway. Courage was dealing with your fears and not letting them rule you."

<u>Activity:</u> The Feelings Check. Staying with an uncomfortable feeling gives an opportunity to stretch and grow. Think of being afraid to speak out. Stay with whatever comes up and breathe deeply. Learn all you can about your body's reaction and the discomfort you experience.

Hang out with the feeling and take deep breaths. Name it: fear, uncertainty, anxiety or uncomfortable and observe how your body tenses up. Notice how uncertainty keeps you from taking risks. Tell yourself that you are a real, live human being with feelings and that's a great thing to be.

Dealing with your bad feelings is like going through a door that you are afraid to open. That door of fear is often only a phantom one anyway, so go ahead and face it, take a deep breath for courage and then walk right through it. You won't bump your head on it! I promise! Fear loses its strong grip. Finding your courage and doing what you are afraid of increases your self-esteem. Courage is facing a short-term discomfort to gain long-term peace. Courage is facing your fear because it is the right thing to do and acting in a way that would make you proud.

<u>Activity:</u> Performance Fears. Here's a man who faces his biggest fear of not being good enough and not believing in himself as he auditions for X-Factor in England. Listen to the strength of his feelings as he overcomes his fear. http://www.youtube.com/watch?v=k1T9-I3wx8I

<u>Activity:</u> Watch the video of Sara Barreilles singing Brave.
http://www.youtube.com/watch?v=QUQsqBqxoR4

A High Powered Life

Know what you stand for.

Know what is right.

Breathe into your highest wisdom.

Act with courage.

Say what you need to hear.

Say it. Do it. Be it.

Clip art © www.djinkers.com

CAGING THE STRESS MONSTER

Objective: To break into stressful thoughts that make you feel out of control.

Dialogue: Melt downs are extreme behaviors you have when you are stressed like crying, having a tantrum or throwing and breaking things. Melt downs aren't any fun. It feels terrible to become anxious and fall apart. Sometimes so much is going on that you worry too much and feel overwhelmed. Let's turn these worries into a big pretend Stress Monster that you can lock up and throw away the key. Close your eyes and imagine what stress might look like if it were a monster. What color would it be? How big would it be? Would it have horns or big teeth? I'll draw what my Stress Monster looks like on the board. How do you see yours?

Activity: Draw a picture of your own personal stress monster. Put words about the stressors that make you feel overwhelmed such as being bullied, parents fighting, mean people, trouble learning something new, too much homework, troubles at home, friends being upset with you, too many bad feelings, etc. Draw a cage around the Stress Monster with bars over it.

Negative thoughts that make you feel helpless make your Stress Monster grow bigger. What do you say to make your own troubles bigger than they really are? (List helpless phrases such as "I can't take this anymore" on the board.) These are victim words—they make you want to give up and stop trying. Stop melt downs before they happen by using deep breathing and using your Thought Stoppage to send victim words away, etc.

Build up your Stress Muscles by pushing yourself a little bit at a time to handle harder and harder situations. It's like lifting weights—you start small and build up until you can handle a great deal. As you move through each difficult situation, you learn how strong you are. By dealing with stress successfully again and again, you build up your stress muscles. Then you can pat yourself on the back for learning something that not everyone knows.

Sometimes you are the one who causes stress for others. Who gets upset with you? What do people look like when they feel stressed? Sometimes you might act like a Stress Monster doing things that puts stress on someone else. Stop and think. Do you tease others when you know that they don't like it? Do you put off doing your homework upsetting your parents? Do you delay doing your chores until somebody yells at you? Your stopping bugging your brother or sister or picking fights because it feels like fun might make everyone in your family happier. You can prevent other people's stress and your own as well by doing things that you need to do when asked the first time even though you don't want to. Your cooperating at home will decrease the amount of stress in your family.

Helper Words:
I catch myself making my Stress Monster bigger and cut it out!
I figure out what stresses me so I can deal with it better.
I feel proud that I can figure out what stresses me and deal with it.
I tell myself, "Let's do this. Let's put these stressors behind bars."

Tips for parents and teachers: Children today are stressed. Keep reminding your children to use Helper Words by modeling them yourself. Constant repetition of these Helper Words in your household or classroom helps a child make the positive messages his or her own. They help reprogram the child's mind to be productive. They create self-empowerment by reinforcing positive ways of thinking and acting.

"Been in a snarky mood lately?

**Don't get left behind by staying
in a grumpy mood that
makes you miserable.**

Get the "ouch" out of Grouch.

**Shift your gears to a "Can Do"
state of mind.**

**Challenge those negative thoughts
that pulls you down.**

**Feel Good Now! Challenge
that Grouch that wants to
take over your mind."**

Lynne Namka   angriesout.com

ROARING BAD THOUGTS AWAY

<u>Objective:</u> To recognize and challenge thoughts that encourage risky behavior.

<u>Dialogue:</u> Some of your thoughts are dangerous trying to trick you into getting in trouble. Some roads are dangerous ones to go down. They are like a villain in a movie—the bad guy who sneaks in to cause trouble. These thoughts are bad characters—the Baddies— who try to get you to do harmful and risky things that send you down a dangerous road. Do you need the Baddies in your mind trying to hijack it? If you correct your mind and toss out the bad thoughts, you will feel better.

Treacherous thoughts double cross you to try to get you in trouble. Let's list some thoughts that might tempt boys and girls to do something that might be harmful or dangerous. (Write three categories of dangerous thoughts that might cause harm on the board: Yourself, your body or someone else—lying, disrespectful, stealing, smoking, crime, drinking etc.)

Watch out when you are in a grouchy mood. Challenge and interrupt any dangerous thought that makes things unsafe for you or others. Thought Stoppage techniques interrupt harmful and perilous thoughts.

<u>Activity:</u> (Role play a skit of chasing the negative thought away by roaring at it. Have a child act out thinking about something dangerous while you as the bad thought come sneaking in and try to tempt him or her. If you physically can, your crawling in to represent the sneaky thought will delight the children. Have the other child roar and say, "Get out of here you Baddie! I'm not going down that Danger Road!" and you run away looking scared.)

Bad choices can leave you feeling down. Sometimes your energies get stuck when you are feeling discouraged. Tap many times on the back of your hand between your little finger and then tap your ring finger. Breathe deeply in and out as you tap. Think about being strong and letting go of thoughts that might cause you harm. If you find your mind telling you to do something you know is wrong, picture what the consequences might be. Then picture yourself roaring while you say "Whenever I'm going down that Danger Road of my mind, I say Whoa! Don't go for something sure-fire stupid."

<u>Helper Words</u>
I give myself a break from my bad thoughts.
I chase unhappy thoughts away by roaring at them, "Get out of here!"
I correct my mind and the rest of my life falls in place.
I'm not going down that sure-fire stupid Danger Road.

<u>Tips for parents and teachers:</u> People are at a different level of being ready to change their own behavior. Habits of a lifetime can become ingrained but they can change with effort. Children listen to what you say. Give repeated messages of saying no to themselves and not giving in to quick feel-good solutions. If young people do not set enough boundaries for themselves in the areas that they find addictive, they use them to produce feel-good neurotransmitters in their brain to feel better. Then they become under the control of these neurotransmitters when doing addictive behaviors and must do more of the unproductive activity to feel better. One antidote to this is to teach your children to become excited over small acts that affect their self-esteem through viewing themselves as someone who can grow and learn and make a difference in their world.

Treacherous thoughts double cross me
to try to get me in trouble.

Thought Stoppage techniques
interrupt harmful thoughts.

I chase unhappy thoughts away by
roaring at them, "Get out of here!"

I challenge negative thoughts with force
and the rest of my life falls in place.

You're going to see me Roar!

I'm not going down that
sure-fire stupid Danger Road.

RIPPING UP TRASH THOUGHTS

Objective: To learn discard negative thoughts.

Dialogue: Unwanted Thoughts? Sometimes ugly thoughts sneak into your thinking. Here are some more ideas about how to get rid of them. Call unwanted, intrusive thoughts "trash thoughts" and throw them away. One study showed that when people wrote negative thoughts down, ripped the paper up and threw them in the trash, the thoughts decreased.

Activity: Throwing Negative Thoughts in the Trash. Let's do something to take charge of what sneaky things your mind comes up with when you are discouraged or tired. It is your mind and you have the right to make it happy. Too much garbage piling up in your mind? Write the negative thoughts down and rip them up then throw them in the trash. You can send ideas and words you don't like to the dumpster.

After taking out the trash, put in something happy in your mind. Pretend something happy is coming in through the top of your head. What makes you smile and feel cheerful? A happy memory? Golden light? Blessings from above? A beautiful color? You get to choose what happy ideas come into your mind. Throw out the old and bring something bright and colorful in. Negative out—happy in.

Do you yell at yourself when you've done something dumb? Do you scold yourself a lot? Unhappy thoughts can pull you down and make you sad. Would you stay with a channel on the TV that pulls your mood down? Change the mental channel of your mind with Thought Stoppage. If you think too much about something being unfair, tell yourself, "I need to stop thinking about unfairness now. I've thought about this enough. I won't buy into this situation. Stop it!"

Activity: Sometimes your brain gets overly emotional when you are angry or anxious. Thinking happy thoughts changes your brain. Endorphins are those good brain chemicals that come when you are having a good time or thinking about happy things. Here's a video cartoon with a picture of those good endorphins that make you more cheerful.

 (This video about anger and endorphins is at www.youtube.com/watch?v=WkKLz61RHXo or at http://www.angriesout.com/raven_flash/angries_01_alternate.html

Give your brain an endorphin charge by being kind to yourself and others. Happy people increase the endorphins in their brain through healthy activities and hobbies. Unhappy young people are more likely to turn to things like gangs, drugs and crime. Make the decision now to keep your mind positive by challenging those ideas that make you feel bad about yourself. When you get older and see me, remind me of the day when you decided that you are in charge of being a happier person.

Tips for parents and teachers: Children learn to deal with stress from their families. Research shows that there is an intergenerational style of coping with adversity and stress in families which can be either positive or negative. Reinforce your own positive ways of thinking out loud so your children will learn to be more confident about overcoming whatever they have to face in life.

Anger is one reaction to an event that represents a personal stressor, threat or loss. You make yourself angry by thinking about how you have been hurt.

Take responsibility for your feelings.

Instead of saying, "He/she/they make me feel _____" remember it is your feeling.

No one else is inside your head making you feel angry.

Instead of saying "My mom makes me angry when _____," say, "I make myself angry when _____."

Choices. You always have a choice what to do with your feelings.

Tell yourself, "I can choose to be upset, try to resolve the problem or let go of my feelings.

You are as mature as you are responsible for owning your thoughts, feelings and behavior.

Lynne Namka   Your Quick Anger Makeover   angriesout.com

WORKING WITH THE AMYGDALA-THE STRESS CENTER IN THE BRAIN

Objective: To learn about how stressful thoughts can change the chemicals in the brain and gene expression.

Dialogue: Words can literally change your brain. Words have the power to change how your brain is functioning. Now science shows that happy and unhappy words influence the expression of genes that regulate physical and emotional stress.

Genes are the part of you that carries information passed on by your Mum and Dad, and your ancestors. Genes are carried by your DNA on your chromosomes. Your genes have markers on them that decide everything about you and how your body works – your hair and skin color, how you respond to stress, how your muscles work, and how you deal with illness.

Gene markers that influence health are turned on when you keep your mind positive. Thinking "I can and I will" thoughts turn on the motivational centers of your brain into action and will build resiliency.

Constant worry and anxiety thoughts increase the activity of the fear center in your brain—the amygdala producing stress hormones. Unhappy thoughts disrupt the specific gene production of positive chemicals that protect us from stress. When you have angry thoughts and words, you go out of the rational and reasoning part of your brain to the alarm center that makes you want to run away or fight.

Angry and unhappy words can send alarm messages through the brain and interrupt the specific genes that produce the positive chemicals that protect you from stress. Angry words take you out of the rational,-reasoning centers in the front part of the brain to the older, primal brain that are wired to protect you.

Using positive words will help change your perception of yourself and the people you interact with. A positive view of yourself will help you see the good in others. Over time your brain changes in response to what you think and say.

Activity: Learning about the Body's Anxiety Switch. There is a small part of your brain called the Amygdala that switches on when you become too emotional or too stressed. Let's watch the video Calm down and Relax the Amygdala. We can stop the video and practice the different breathing techniques. http://www.youtube.com/watch?v=Zs559guIGDo

Change your words and transform your reality. Change the inner soup of chemicals in your brain and make a happy brain soup by thinking loving thoughts and doing stress management techniques.

Tips for parents and teachers: More can be found on how genes work can be found at http://www.cyh.com/HealthTopics/HealthTopicDetailsKids.aspx?p=335&np=152&id=2287. Just for Kids: A Cartoon Guide to Genes and how they form us is at: http://history.nih.gov/exhibits/genetics/kids.htm

The hardest
storms are the
ones that help you
grow.

Keep on walking.
Keep your feet
a moving.
Hold your head
up high.

Walk through
that storm.

You won't be the
same person who
walked in.

106

BECOME HAPPIER BY RECOGNIZING YOUR SIGNATURE STRENGTHS

<u>Objective:</u> To acknowledge one's better qualities and increase them.

<u>Dialogue:</u> You have strong positive qualities and ways of acting that make up who you are. A Signature Strength is a strong point that you have that helps you be the best you can be. Look over this list of positive advantages that you have in your personality. Acknowledge your strengths and build upon them. They help you do well in dealing with the real world. Values are those characteristics that you hold worthwhile because they are the real you. You make choices daily from your values, so know your standards, interests and principles. When you know what you stand for, you can make conscious decisions and better direct the course of your life.

<u>Activity:</u> Let's learn who you are and what you stand for. What abilities do you have that make you a better person? Take an inventory of your own strengths. Underline several of your top Signature Strengths on the chart. Think of an example of each. Think about each one and how it plays out in your life.

Got Happiness? Get More! See a cartoon video on Positive Psychology at http://www.youtube.com/watch?v=hFk3abxjwCg

For older children see a white board animation cartoon called What is Positive Psychology? at http://www.youtube.com/watch?v=1qJvS8v0TTI

Now for some Happiness Plus. Identify a new strength you would like to increase in your life. Then decide what actions you could take to increase the quality and quantity of this trait each day. Again, practice, practice, practice these strengths until they are a part of who you are! The more you practice a new habit, the better you become at it. Get these new ways of thinking installed in your brain with super glue-stick tightness.

Let's watch the first 40 seconds of this video to reinforce what really makes people happy in life. http://www.youtube.com/watch?v=IP4Pgbqjjlg. (The rest of the video is on EFT which is a marvelous technique for releasing negative memories and emotions.)

If you want to have a good character, motivate yourself to do what it takes to become a person you admire and respect. Your good sense of yourself as a caring and productive person "slips" away when you see yourself as being less than worthy. Addictions like drinking, smoking and doing drugs also cause a slippage of character as you focus more and more on the addictive substance or activity instead of on the good things that create a happy life.

<u>Tips for parents and teachers:</u> Visualizing a goal helps children spend more time going after it. According to the motivational research, impulsive people often think only of the present. They feel unhappy or bored when they have to wait for gratification. Visualizing and anticipating about a future reward turns on excitement and correspondingly the pleasure center in the brain. Research showed that excitement grew in impulsive people as they got closer to their reward.

The Six Virtues and Twenty-four Character Strengths

1. Wisdom and knowledge   **Cognitive strengths to acquire and use knowledge**

Creativity   Thinking of new, productive ways to do things
Curiosity   Taking an interest in new experiences
Open-mindedness   Thinking things through. Seeing them from all sides
Love of learning   Mastering new skills and topics of knowledge
Perspective   Giving wise advice to others

2. Courage   **Standing up against wrong doing**

Authenticity   Speaking the truth and being genuine
Bravery   Not shrinking from threat, difficulty or pain
Persistence   Perseverance. Finishing what you start
Zest   Approaching life with excitement and energy

3. Humanity   **Impersonal strengths for tending and befriending others**

Kindness   Doing favors and good deeds for others
Love   Valuing close relations with others
Social Intelligence   Being aware of motives and feelings of self and others

4. Justice   **Being involved in a healthy community life**

Fairness   Treating all people the same and being fair
Leadership   Organizing and making group activities happen
Teamwork   Working well as a member of a group or team

5. Temperance   **Strengths that protect against many harmful behaviors**

Forgiveness   Forgiving those who have done wrong
Modesty   Letting one's accomplishments speak for themselves
Prudence   Making careful choices; not doing harmful things

6. Transcendence
meaning   **Making connections to the universe and finding**

Excellence and beauty appreciation   Noticing beauty, excellence and performance

Gratitude   Being thankful for the good things that happen
Hope   Expecting the best and working to achieve it
Humor   Smiling, liking to laugh and having fun with others
Religiousness   Loving beliefs of higher purpose and meaning of life

(Adapted for children from Seligman, et. al. Positive Psychology Progress, American Psychologist.)

GROWTH MINDSET: WHEN IT'S HARD, KEEP ON GOING

<u>Objective</u>: To learn that how you think determines the motivation to do hard work.

<u>Dialogue:</u> What kind of life do you want to have? Do you want to have an exciting life where you are in charge of who you become? You and only you get to plan how you want your future to be. The best way to have a happy, fulfilled future is to give yourself a growth mindset! A growth mindset means that you believe that you can do learn and grow through hard work and effort. It puts you in charge by wiping out the self-limiting beliefs that hold you back. Believe that you can do something challenging and you are half way there. If you think you can do something and are willing to work hard, the chances are good that you can. Believing that you can change is called growth mindset. Growth mindset people thrive under pressure.

A fixed mindset is the belief that you can't change. It is having the belief that your intelligence or talent are fixed and that you can't improve through practice and hard work. People with fixed mindsets say, "I'm not good at this. It's too hard. I don't care about this stuff. It's boring. Why bother?" You talk yourself out of trying challenging yourself to accomplish something. People with fixed mindsets are afraid of risking and being wrong. One of our greatest fears is the fear of being wrong and being found out by others. Fixed mindsets cause people to fold or fall apart.

<u>Activity:</u> Watch and discuss this Fixed vs. Growth Mindsets in Children You Tube video about how beliefs stop you from taking risks www.youtube.com/watch?v=UNAMrZr9OWY

Our brains are like stretchy plastic—this is called Neuroplasticity. Your brain can be made stronger by pushing yourself to try new ways and even fail so that you can learn from mistakes. Your intelligence can be improved through learning. Your skills and talents will get better if you work hard at improving them. If something is hard to learn at first, you are learning and stretching your brain. People with fixed mindsets who say discouraging things don't stretch their brains to be the best it can be. If you want to enlarge your brain and achieve success in life, get a growth mindset! How you think determines who you become. So learn to be successful when you fail by learning.

The opposite is also true. If you think you can't, you can't. The good news is you can change your mindset so you can handle pressure! It's not enough to have a gift or talent or extra smarts. You have to develop yourself. Even smart people for whom learning comes easily can set themselves up to fail. If you think you are special because you are smart and don't have to work hard, that may be true now. But at some point, like when you go to high school or college and hit a hard subject, you won't have the tools for dealing with frustration and pushing yourself through the hard work. Then when you take a subject that is hard for you to do, you will be more likely to give up.

Hard stuff to learn and do will always be there. Wanting only to do easy work is a trap of fixed mindset thinking. With easy work, you don't challenge yourself. Your brain does not build new neural networks. Having the belief that you can be lazy and slack off on tough tasks locks you into not trying when things do get hard. Don't let this type of slacker thinking deceive you.

<u>Helper Words:</u>
I'm no slacker. I push myself through to get the prize.
I have the problem-solving brain.
My brain says, "Come on; give me something tough to tackle so I can grow!"

Open Your Mind to New Possibilities!

Growth Mindset is the coolest attitude of all!

**Pushing through hard learning tasks
builds confidence.**

**Give yourself an awesome attitude to
max out your brain!**

**A growth mindset is knowing you can grow
and learn through hard work and effort.**

**A growth mindset gives you
positive strategies and tools.**

Believing in yourself makes you a winner for life!

You become what you want to be by your choices.

**Practice every day being your very best self
and that's what you will become.**

Choosing the best tools for your brain is Totally Rad!

Clip art © www.djinkers.com

HOW YOUR BRAIN LEARNS NEW PATHWAYS

Objective: To learn to bypass uncomfortable feelings of embarrassment and shame.

Dialogue: Do you want to look smart to others so you try to hide your mistakes? Do you like school work best when it is easy or when it forces you to stretch your brain? Learning something new that is hard might be frustrating and you might feel uncomfortable. Do you sometimes feel stupid and want to take the easy way out when you make a mistake? Uh oh! That's fixed mindset thinking that needs to be challenged and turned around. Don't run or hide from your errors just because you feel dumb. Mistakes can be treasures when you learn from them.

Activity: Catch that feeling you get when you want to hide something you've done. You know that feeling, we've all had it; you're embarrassed that you goofed up and don't want anyone to know. It is a feeling of shame based on a belief of "I'm not good enough." It's just a feeling to be learned from. Feelings are temporary and they are just feelings. Don't protect yourself from uncomfortable feelings when learning something new.

Fixed mindset people believe that if they have high ability and learn easily, they shouldn't have to work hard at something. Some people who are smart or talented might think "I shouldn't have to work like other people." They have the mistaken idea that they can coast along and not develop themselves. Fixed mindset people are more likely be tempted to cheat on a test and lie about their accomplishments because they want to look good. They pass up the opportunity to feel good about mastering new skills. People who focus on superficial things build bigger pathways in their brain that don't get them anywhere. Although they often deny it, deep down within, they can hold a lot of shame because they have let themselves become lazy.

The harder you work at something, the better you will be at it. Enjoying giving good effort will build those brain muscles. The key to success in life is to do things that you fear or that are hard. Struggling to get something makes more brain cells. We should be saying, "This is too easy for me. Give me something hard so I can grow more neurons." You don't have to feel dumb if you don't get something the first time. When you struggle with a difficult task, you are getting smarter. You can grow your brain like a muscle.

Activity: There is a part of our brains that deals with errors. Scientist took brain scans of people with the growth mindsets while they were making errors. The anterior cingulate cortex in their brains lit up as they made the mistake and tried to figure out what went wrong. Fixed mindset people did not show activity in their brains when they made mistakes. Here's a video of how the brain learns new pathways at http://www.youtube.com/watch?v=cgLYkV689s4

Brain science about resilience shows that when you learn new things and push yourself, you increase the neural networks in your brain. Your brain stretches and grows every time you take on a challenge. Your brain works harder when you try to figure out what went wrong and then try another way. Work out your brain just like it is a muscle you want to make bigger. Push out of your comfort zone and your brain will form new connections and you will get smarter.

.

111

GROWTH MINDSET

Effort and perseverance.

Asking questions and taking criticism.

Holding the focus.

Ignoring distractions.

Trying different strategies.

Pride of work.

Buckling down.

Stretching your smart brain.

Growing your Intelligence.

Bring-it-on Attitude.

Happy Mindset. Happy Brain.

Happy Life!

CHALLENGE THAT FIXED MINDSET

<u>Objective</u>: To break into any unconscious beliefs about not being able to change.

<u>Dialogue</u>: Your mind is like a computer that has certain programs installed in it. When you were smaller you may have made up your mind that you weren't good at some things and stopped trying. You installed a negative fixed mindset software program. An intervention is when you do what it takes to turn your life around. You intervene or break into something you want to change. Families do interventions sometimes to get someone stop drinking or doing drugs. You can do something to stop those behaviors that don't work for you. You can uninstall beliefs that don't work.

<u>Activity</u>: Tap It Out. Tapping interventions are easy to do by tapping all over your body from the back of your neck, up over your head, around your ears and down the rest of your body. You hit many different acupressure points in the different meridians when you do random tapping all over your body. You can tap out fixed mindset ideas.

Sometimes we hold on to negative beliefs about ourselves because we don't believe that we can change. Negative beliefs are to be challenged, not ignored. So let's confront common unproductive beliefs that many people have. Forgiving yourself for having these beliefs is a major step to change. Strong emotions cause your body to be out of balance. Forgiving yourself about having human feelings will assist you in becoming the best person you can be. Forgiveness gives you freedom to let go of the old and bring in the new and improved you. Forgiveness is love in action.

Take a long, slow deep breath and say I forgive myself and I'm a good person," while we tap:

Even though I believe I can't change because _____,
Even though I made a decision about not being able to change,
Even though I have a fixed mindset about _____,
Even though I gave up when it was hard and I felt _____,
Even though I was frustrated when learning _____ was hard and gave up,
Even though I told myself that I can't because I'm not _____,
Even though I told myself that I was no good and it was no use,
Even though I told myself that _____ was boring,
Even though I gave up too easily before I even tried,
Even though I have held myself back by believing _____,
Even though I decided I didn't like school when_____,
Even though I felt hopeless about _____ and stopped trying,
Even though I feel sad that I've held myself back by believing _____,
Even though I'm still not good at _____,

Take a deep breath and let it out slowly. How do you feel now? Do you feel more relaxed, energized or open and hopeful? Forgiving yourself and making the decision to do better in the future is a sure-fire way to open up your mind to new possibilities.

<u>Tips for parents and teachers</u>: Tapping all over while owning the problem and then saying the correction can balance the body's energy. Try this on yourself. Tapping turns on the good endorphins and creates more of a balance between the right and left sides of the brain.

Fixed Mindset is About Fear.

Fear that you can't do something.

Fear of feeling uncomfortable inside.

Fear of looking dumb to others.

Fear of working hard.

Fear of making mistakes.

Fear that you can't change.

Insecurity beliefs stop

you in your tracks.

They give you a boring life

Do not let your fears dumb you down.

Do not Feed the Fears!

Don't be Scared!

Clip art © www.djinkers.com

TAPPING IN NEW GROWTH MINDSET IDEAS

<u>Objective:</u> To strengthen new ideas for change that promote learning and growth.

<u>Materials:</u> Post It Notes.

<u>Dialogue:</u> We all have things that we are not good at and give up on. Think about forgiveness which is a tremendous concept. Forgiving yourself for what you did that didn't work and making the decision to become different sets the stage for change.

<u>Activity:</u> Watch this video by Mateusz M. on Why Do We Fall? Listen to the idea that you like best. http://www.youtube.com/watch?v=mgmVOuLgFB0 Which idea appealed to you?

Write the ideas down on these Post It notes that you liked so you put them on your mirror at home. Write these ideas on the front of your notebooks. Program your mind with these positive ideas. Your mind is just like a computer that can learn new programs. When you want to program in big changes, tap all over your body while taking deep breaths. Your brain will turn on good endorphins, your body will relax and your unconscious mind will decide to take on these positive ways of thinking. Challenge your excuses and negative thinking. Use positive thoughts to hold on to your dreams. Have big dreams and grow yourself into them.

<u>Activity:</u> Watch this Awakening video by Mateusz M. that asks you to challenge yourself to stop saying "But I tried it and it didn't work" and make a firm decision to step into your fears and live your life in an exciting manner. http://www.youtube.com/watch?v=WDf757QwXpk

<u>Activity:</u> Having growth mindset ideas firmly planted in your life will give you an awesome future. Repeat these growth mindset words while we tap on our faces and bodies to tap in positive ideas.

I believe in myself and in my ability to grow and change and stretch my brain.
I have the potential to shift any belief that I choose. Beliefs are just beliefs.
Just because I believed something bad about myself doesn't mean that it is true. It was just a belief.
I own negative thoughts that cross my mind and throw them out.
I watch and interrupt any negative thoughts about _____,
I am open to examining new areas of my life where I limit myself. (lack of will power, procrastination, feelings of boredom and anxiety about failing)
I push myself through feelings of dread and fear of failure.
I remind myself that I'm strong and feelings of frustration will not stop me.
I come up with strategies that will keep me from being distracted.
I cheer myself on when the going gets tough.
Change is not always easy but it is possible when I put my mind to it.
I am excited about changing my fixed mindset beliefs.
I chose to believe that I am unlimited in my ability to learn. The sky is the limit.

Hope for the best that you can be and then make that hope a reality. Now think about hope and how would be if you lived by these growth mindset ideas. You would be one fantastic person! You are in charge of your mind. Believe in your ability to become the best you can be. Hope keeps you in the game!

Fear of failure is the greatest dream stopper of all!

Humiliation and embarrassment are feelings of fear.

But hey, they are just feelings.

Face your feelings and set yourself soaring!

Magic happens when you face your fear of being wrong.

Stand tall, look fear in the face and say,

"I'm going after my dreams.

I'm so done with you.

You don't run me anymore."

MAMIMIZE YOUR BRAIN

<u>Objective</u>: To learn that the brain is flexible and can grow new neural pathways.

<u>Dialogue</u>: Downer words stop you dead in your tracks. Fixed mindsets are full of discouraging words to fool you and pull you down to keep you from becoming your best self and having good things come to you. Why do you need to learn about your brain? What do you do when you have a hard lesson to learn? Do you push on like a steam roller or dumb yourself down and say things to make yourself give up? Think about the last hard thing you had to learn. Did you get it done? What did you say to yourself to keep on going or shut down and turn off?

<u>Activity</u>: Watch the Brainology video about how your brain works on YouTube at http://www.youtube.com/watch?v=pF5yB31IT5Y

Think of something that is hard for you that you have given up on. What fixed mindset words did you tell yourself? You get to choose the type of words that you put in your brain. Downer Words pull you down. "Can Do" words boost your mood and give your energy. Remember the rule of practicing new habits. The more you practice breaking into those Downer words and replacing them with "Can Do" words, the happier you'll become. Good habits become routine when you repeat them many times.

<u>Fixed mindsets—Downer Words</u>
I give up. This is too hard.
I like easy work and lot of praise.
I don't want to feel bad inside so I avoid hard work.
I switch off when the task is tough.
I want to look good instead of working hard.

All beliefs come forth from within your mind. Good stuff. Bad stuff. Good stuff you can keep. Bad stuff you can change. The truth is that you are a beautiful person who may have felt humiliated when you were younger. But shame and humiliation are not who you are. You are much, much more than your painful emotions. It's not a mistake if you learn something from it. 'Fess up. It's not so bad. You may feel bad for a moment but you'll get relief in the long run. Make new mistakes— not the same old ones over and over. Make good mistakes—those ones that you can learn from! Being able to admit that you did something wrong is called growth.

<u>Helper Words for the "Can Do" Attitude</u>
I feel good about thriving on challenge.
I ignore others who are goofing off.
I like feedback on how I did as it helps me grow.
If I can't get something, I try harder.
If I think I can, I can. If I do, my brain stretches and grows!

<u>Tips for parents and teachers</u>: A video overview of the Brainology curriculum is at http://www.youtube.com/watch?v=sF9fEgHzhhQ Children with fixed mindsets can grow up to be slackers and failures in life as they give up easily when things become hard for them. Children need growth mindset strategies to help them overcome the crashes and collapses that life sometimes brings. Your own belief in having the choice to change things about one's self will motivate your children to become winners in life.

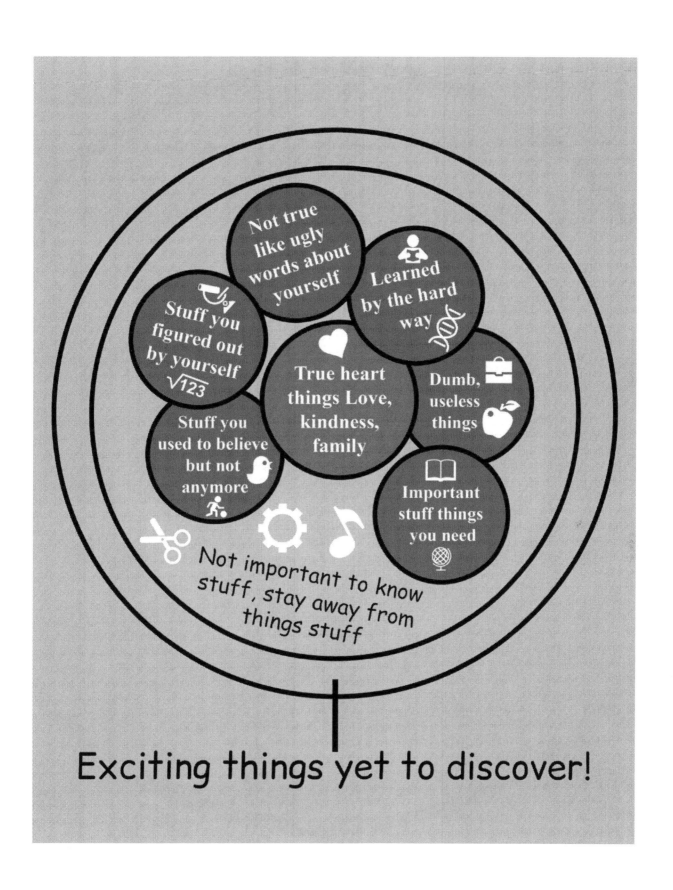

Exciting things yet to discover!

SENDING DOWNER WORDS TO THE DUMP

<u>Objective:</u> Interrupting fixed mindset words.

<u>Dialogue:</u> Sometimes when we are young we learn things that are wrong that make us feel bad about ourselves. We pick up mistaken ideas and beliefs about ourselves that are harmful for us. They are left over ideas and unresolved feelings from our past and have not yet discarded.

Sometimes you need to let go of old things that no longer fit you. You let go of old toys we no longer play with and pass on old clothes, yet sometimes you might hold on to outgrown beliefs that make you feel bad about yourselves. Downer Beliefs stop you dead in your tracks and keep you from moving forward. They are negative, negative, negative! Fixed mindsets are full of Downer Beliefs. When you think about them instead of doing your work, you give up easily.

Don't catch yourself in a trap of never being able to change and grow. It keeps you just as you are without hope of change. Listen to yourself when you don't want to do your homework. What do you say to yourself just before you give up on something hard? Let's make a list of Stopper Words that pull you down so you can watch out for them.

I can't. It's too hard.	It's impossible. I can't change.
It's not fair.	What's the point?
It won't make a difference.	I'm no good.
I give up (without giving it your best.)	It doesn't matter (when it does.)
They don't care so I don't care.	Life is not fair.
I don't deserve good things.	I'm not good at this.

You can set a goal and then break it down into small steps and feel good as you get each step done. Goals are easier if you give up your Downer Words. Which of these words do you need to throw out? Stop thinking about all the reasons it won't work and think of the one reason it will. Attitude is everything. When you question yourself about whether you can do a hard job or not, tell yourself, Yes, I can!"Thinking that you can't do things sets up a chronic negative attitude. Negativity sets you up to be not pleased, not happy and not powerful. You and only you are the only one who is in charge of your attitude. Turn your "I can'ts" into "I can!"

<u>Activity:</u> How to Be Number One. Let's watch this video on the famous Notre Dame Coach, Vince Lombardi. Lombardi later went on to be the coach of the Green Bay Packers.
http://www.youtube.com/watch?v=UpBKzjkpX0Y

You can't solve your problem with the same thinking that got you there in the first place. Tell yourself that the work is a challenge you can do it. Coach yourself when work is hard and pep talk yourself into getting the job done. When faced with something hard, remind yourself, "I can do this. I will do what needs to be done today." There is no substitute for hard work. I say "Let's do this. Let's get it done.

<u>Helper Words:</u>
I refuse to talk myself into becoming a loser. I throw out Stopper Words.
I'm stressing myself out big time. I've gotta stop fixed mindset thinking.
I tell myself, "I can do this!" I get lots done when I put my mind to a task.
I set small goals and feel satisfaction getting one step done at a time.

DOWNER WORD :
IF YOU THINK YOU CAN'T
YOU ARE RIGHT

BE YOUR OWN COACH

<u>Objective</u>: To learn to give yourself good advice when going through hard times.

<u>Dialogue</u>: Sometimes life gives you a raw deal. Unhappy events pop up. Tough things happen to you and your family. Homework gets tougher to do. Or you might have trouble learning something new. Fixed mindset thinking will keep you frozen in the bad situation. Do you say these fixed mindset things that people say to make them get discouraged, depressed and give up?

I can't.	I'm overwhelmed.	I hate this.
It's terrible!	It's too hard.	I'm so stressed.
I'm no good.	This is dumb.	I don't have to do this.

Resilient boys and girls look for new ways of thinking and acting to make themselves strong by keeping a growth mindset. They find new strategies to deal with upsets and problems. They stop doing old ways of acting that do not work. They throw out the word "can't" and replace it with "I can and I will because I'm worth it."

You can make yourself weak or strong by what you tell yourself. You can make yourself able to thrive and deal with pressure. When going through some hard task, keep on going. Don't bog yourself down in a muddle of helpless thoughts. Tell yourself, "When push comes to shove, I deal with my situation. I push and shove myself through the bad times. There are better times coming ahead if I keep my mind positive."

<u>Activity</u>: Becoming Your Own Best Coach. Sometimes you get stuck in a rut and don't know what to do. That's when you need to call in that Coach who tells you what you need to hear. Sometimes you need a different way of looking at the problem. Shift your thinking. Think of a coach that helped you improve your game. Really good coaches use a lot of Helper Words. Great coaches say a lot of "Attaboys" and "Attagirls." They also give you feedback on your performance. What did a coach tell you that made you feel good and keep on working? Let's list some of these "Good Coach Words" on the board. "Get your A game on! Push yourself outside your comfort zone."

Watch this motivational video of Will Smith talking to his son from the movie The Pursuit of Happyness. Pretend that Will Smith was your coach. What might he say to you?
http://www.mentormob.com/learn/i/positive-messages-growth-mindsets/youtube-will-smith-motivational-pursuit-of-happyness

When you are discouraged, remember to coach yourself. Tell yourself that you are a hard-working person who can pull your weight to make a good effort. You are a strong person who can handle hard work with confidence. Confidence is being able to fail and bounce back after a tough time. That turns your failure into a success! A failure is something that doesn't work; it is never a person. Believe in your ability to improve on new things with hard work. Coach yourself through stressful times. Acknowledge your strengths but also recognize your weak areas and ratchet up your effort.

<u>Helper Words</u>
I try, try again in a different way when I get stuck.
I won't be afraid of risking and failing.
I won't fold under pressure. I'll thrive!
I tell myself that I'm a hard worker and that makes me feel good.

BEING FLEXIBLE DURING STORMY TIMES

<u>Objective</u>: To learn to have an open, flexible mind to deal with problems.

<u>Dialogue</u>: Everybody has stressors of one sort or another. Remember the two kinds of stress—the outside kind and the inside kind? Outside or external stressors are those unpleasant things that happen to you. Let's list these on the board. "Your parent loses a job. Your best friend moves away. Your team loses an important ball game. A relative you love dies. Your mom gets sick." Give me some more examples of outside things that happen.

 Inside stress is the pressure, strain and constant worry that you put on yourselves when something bad has happened. You can't always change outside stressors but you can change how you think about them be become resilient.

Resilience means being tough and strong and being quick to recover when setbacks happen. Have you ever seen a tree dancing and moving in a strong wind? If the tree were stiff, brittle and unbending, it might break from the stressor of the wind. People are the same way. They can bend and be flexible or they can break under pressure. Being resilient means you find the ability to stretch and snap back instead of being rigid and breaking under pressure.

<u>Activity</u>: Dancing and Flowing with the Wind. What favorite Helper Words make you flexible like the willow tree? I'll list them on the board. We will do a play and the person who is the flexible tree can say Helper Words. (Role play this concept of bending and not breaking under stress. Have one child be the rigid tree that breaks or blows over while the other children be the wind blowing from a distance. Then have the child who portrays a rigid tree decide to dance with the wind instead of bracing against it. Pantomime being graceful and flowing and moving with the wind with fluid arm movements with fingers wide open to let the wind through.)

Don't let yourself break like a tree that breaks in a hard wind. Think of a tree blowing in the wind and remind yourself that you are flexible. Tell yourself, "Stress, you will not break me. No fixed mindset thoughts for me. I won't say "Why me?" I'll say 'Try me. I'm tough. I'll work it out."

<u>Activity</u>: Read and discuss the children's book, *On a Beam of Light: The Story of Albert Einstein, Illustrated by Vladimir Radunsky* to learn how Einstein's eccentric behavior helped keep his mind open to the creative process. Albert was an unusual child who said nary a word for his first three years and had trouble learning in school. He then caught up and asked questions, questions and questions! (Discuss how the children think that Einstein became so creative and made his mind flexible to solve important questions.)

<u>Helper Words</u>:
I keep an open mind to go with the flow instead of bracing against it.
I have a flexible mind that shifts gears easily.
I do the work and then feel good for putting in the effort.
If I get down on myself I say, "Enough grousing already. Just do this and get it over".

<u>Tips for parents and teachers</u>: One of the biggest lessons a child needs to learn is how to deal with the feelings of frustration and discouragement that accompany failure and obstacles. Teaching the language of resilience will change your child's view of him or herself. Low levels of resilience are associated with poor self-control, increased mental stress, lack of focus, an inability to manage the social and academic demands of school, a greater likelihood of engaging in risky and/or unhealthy behaviors, poor physical health and less success in school and career.

Lame Excuses Come from Lame Minds

I can't help it. This is just how I am.

I never did like change.

Huh? Why me? Why should I change?

I'm too dumb to change.

Why bother? It's too much trouble.

It's too late for me.

I have a permanent defect. Nothing is
ever going to change that.

I've always been this way and can't change.

Poor me. It's just too hard.

LEARNING TO PERSIST WITH SELF TALK AND HARD WORK

<u>Objective:</u> To learn to persistence and cheer self on.

<u>Dialogue:</u> What does it mean to persist at something? Yes, it means to keep on going, carrying on and sticking with something until it is done. It is determination and stick-to-itness. Who do you know who is persistent? Persistence is a great strength to have.

You can make yourself into a more persistent person. You can get yourself past any idea that you can't do the task if you use Helper Words. If you get discouraged when you find the homework hard, give yourself a good talking to. Remind yourself, "This is a challenge to do my best. I choose to do this because I can. I get a lot done when I put my mind to a task. I set a goal and break it down into small steps that I can achieve. One step at a time and I get where I need to go. I am up to this challenge. I let this challenge change me for the better."

<u>Activity:</u> Persistence Wins the Race. Let's watch a video of Olympian Gold Winner Jesse Owen who took first place in the Olympic Games in Nazi Germany. He persisted and fought the odds and won the race due to his stick-to-itness and became a national hero. http://www.mentormob.com/learn/i/positive-messages-growth-mindsets/youtube-impossible-is-nothing-motivational-video

We all have our own races to run. Persist, persist, persist. Persistence wins the prize. Learning something hard doesn't happen all at once. Sometimes a new thing just doesn't click. You try, try and try and suddenly you get it. It falls into place. Keep on rereading the material and turn it around in your head. While you puzzle over the problems. Ask yourself, "What does that mean? Is there another way to see this? What is the missing piece?"

Remind yourself, "Failure is just another learning experience. I have an opportunity to look at what I did wrong and correct it. I can take risks and make good mistakes that I learn from and that makes me a winner. I can make mistakes into a success." When you fix your thinking, your problems can solve themselves. You do the job, that's all you need to do. Cheer yourself on when the going gets tough. But remember no giving yourself High Fives for doing easy stuff. Save your applause for hard work well done. Believe in effort and you believe in yourself. Heroes are ones who get the hard jobs done.

<u>Helper Words:</u>
I see the bigger goal and break it into small steps and feel great after achieving each step.
I tell myself, "Persistence wins the prize."
I won't say "It's too hard." I say, "I'm tough. I'll work it through."
Wow! Did I do that? Did I actually get that hard work done?

<u>Tips for parents and teachers:</u> Children observe what you do. Little monkey see, little monkey do. You are a prime role model for how you want your children to address problems. Model problem solving by talking out loud and analyzing your mistakes when dealing with a hard task: "I could try this; what would happen? Oh, that doesn't work, maybe if I do this instead. I'll try another way."

We all have our own races to run.

Persist, persist, persist.
Keep on pushing on.
Failure is just another
learning experience.
Persistence wins the prize.
Keep cheering yourself on.
Push yourself to be the
best you can be.

©dianne j. hook

BAD THINGS HAPPEN: DEAL WITH THEM

Objective: To learn to keep moving when going through a bad time.

Dialogue: Problems always come up. That's life. There will be bumps in the road. You will have setbacks in life. Everyone has times when nothing seems to go right. You have to deal with it. One definition of life is Surprise! Surprise; you get some good things! Surprise; you get some bad things! Smart people know that unexpected upsets are temporary and learn ways to get past them. They figure out how to keep on going when things are tough.

What does the word "stride" mean? (Demonstrate what a fast going forward stride is.) So there you are walking down the street just fine getting into your comfortable stride and wham, you are hit with a tough situation. Tough stuff happens, you know? Setbacks can knock you down temporarily. What does it mean "take it in stride?" Successful people pick themselves up, dust themselves off and keep on going.

Activity: Break My Stride. Watch the You Tube music video at http://www.youtube.com/watch?v=8nTeTPZ8RzE

Ain't nothing' gonna break my stride,
Nobody's gonna slow me down, oh-no,
I got to keep on moving
Ain't nothing' gonna break my stride,
I'm running and I won't touch ground
Oh-no, I got to keep on moving!

Stuff happens. It's your job to learn to deal with it. Catch yourself if you start to think fixed mindset thoughts that stress you out and throw you off course. Throw out those old excuses that slow you down and break your stride. Break into any helpless and hopeless things that you tell yourself that pull your mood down such as, "I can't handle this. Why do bad things always happen? This is too hard for me to bear. I give up."

Tips for parents and teachers: Watch your own language when you are hit with financial and social stressors. Your children are listening to what you say and observing how you handle loss and events that seem overwhelming. Research showed that children who had mothers who experienced adverse events from which they had trouble recovering said more defeatist, learned helplessness statements.

FEELING PROUD AFTER DEALING WITH A SETBACK

<u>Objective:</u> To recognize and congratulate one's self for dealing with setbacks.

<u>Materials:</u> Nerf balls or paper to wad up into balls and a piece of heavy cardboard. Write on the Nerf balls or on the paper with a marker typical children's problems written on them such as "family problems, money tight at home, friend not playing with me, being called name, being bullied, getting in trouble, etc."

<u>Dialogue:</u> There are times in life when it seems that nothing is going right for you. Setbacks are devastating only if you think they will last forever. They never do. When you get one of those bad surprise moments, what are you doing to do? Let's pretend that Life is throwing you a curve ball and you get to choose what to do with it.

<u>Activity:</u> Knocking Problems Away. There are problems that might slow you down in life but you can keep your mind on getting through the tough time. Let's practice knocking the problems out of the ball park with this cardboard and practicing Helper Words.

(Have one child pitch the balls one at a time while naming what a setback might be.) Here comes the setback of 'Failing an important test. Here is feeling discouraged. This next one is dealing with a cross dad etc.' Have the batter choose from these Helper Words to feel empowered:

<u>Helper Words:</u>
I tell myself, "Way to go!" and knock my bad thoughts away.
I interrupt my negative thoughts to become a winner!
When Life throws me curve balls, I'll knock them out of the park!
All right! I'll get though this bad time. Things will change. I'll just do it!

After you get through a hard time, you can look back and congratulate yourself for being resilient. Here's what some other boys and girls said about what they learned. Which ones do you like?

I learned to cheer myself on as I worked through that time of my life.
No one deserves to experience what happened to me, but I got through pretty well.
I am a stronger person now and wiser as a result of this experience.
I feel like a better person having looked at those awful feelings.
I know that I am tough and can talk myself through things to survive.
 I am better prepared for whatever comes along.
When my parents divorced, I was scared but I'm less afraid of change now.
I didn't know I could get through a tough time, but I did.
I can help others who have a similar thing to go through.

<u>Tips for parents and teachers:</u> Setbacks and dealing with disappointment are part of life to overcome. Teaching your children how to handle feelings of disappointment will give them skills to spur them on when they face adversity. The ability to deal with a failure event and see it as challenge to learn something new is paramount in motivation. We all have areas where we are not talented; learning ways to motivate oneself to accomplish a difficult but necessary task helps focus the attention and applying more effort.

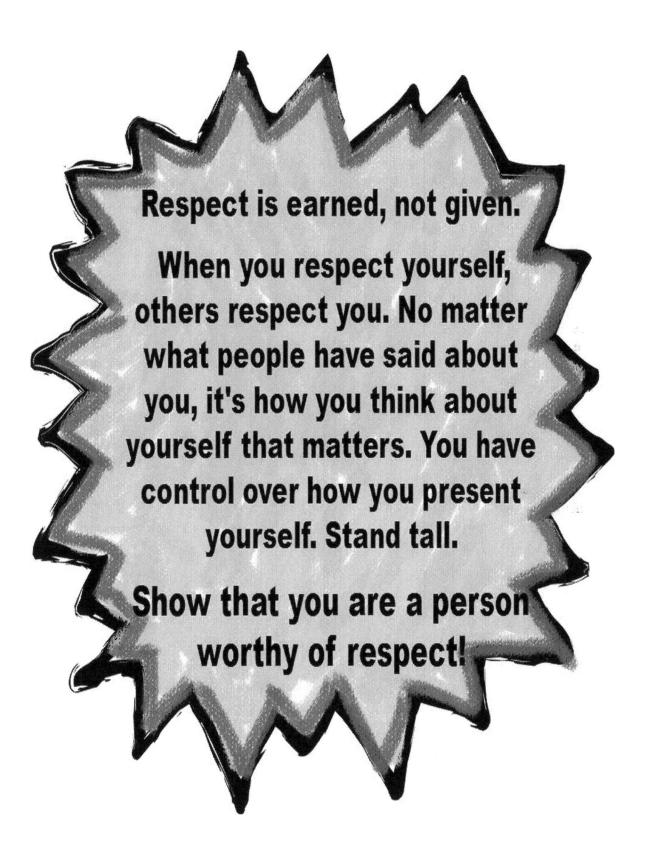

Respect is earned, not given.

When you respect yourself, others respect you. No matter what people have said about you, it's how you think about yourself that matters. You have control over how you present yourself. Stand tall.

Show that you are a person worthy of respect!

130

PERFORMANCE ANXIETY: THE NAVY SEALS FORMULA

Objective: To learn an approach to quell self doubt and performance anxiety.

Dialogue: One of the biggest fears that we have is not doing well on something. Fear of failing is called performance anxiety. People might feel anxious when they have to give a speech or take a test. Did you ever push your panic button when you had to take an important test? Do you scare yourself with "I won't do well" or "I'm going to fail" thoughts?

Activity: The Navy SEALS are deep sea divers who have the challenging task of going under the water to fix problems and recover things. New recruits for the Navy SEALS have to learn to go under water for periods of time. Not being able to breathe in dark, murky water can cause panic. They developed four steps to help stop anxiety and fear and not push the panic button. See yourself starting to panic about something challenging such as a hard test and then do these four steps to calm yourself down.

1. Set your goal. Decide what you want to have happen instead of giving in to your worst fears. Define it well and focus with intensity until you make it happen. Put your focus on what you want instead of being afraid. Prepare by studying hard.

> My goal is to face this with calmness keeping my smarts about me.
> I want to be calm when I face new tasks or tests.
> I'll throw that fear out the window

2. Visualize the situation in your mind. Rehearse what you might say to yourself.

> I visualize myself studying hard and then acing the test.
> If any fear thought comes up, I see myself dismissing it quickly.
> I see myself panicking and then moving through my fears.
> I see myself giving a great performance, then goofing up and recovering quickly.

3. Tell yourself to snap out of it and switch to the "can do" talk to override fear thoughts.

> I've gotten through worse situations and I'm going to get through this.
> Fear is not my master.
> I dismiss my mind chatter about fear.

4. Control your nervousness. Do ten long breaths to calm the parts of your brain that register fear. Push the breath out way down to the bottom of your stomach. Picture yourself succeeding.

> Breathing helps the knowledge in my brain flow out easily.
> I jump up and down and shake my hands to release nervousness.
> I avoid distractions that keep me from my goal of performing well.

That's the four steps. Now switch your thoughts to the positive. Do the switcheroo! Tell yourself that you are excited about what you are about to do. Turn any nervousness and anxiety into excitement! Being excited about your test or speech can give you positive energy. Visualize a positive outcome and tell yourself over and over. "I'm excited. I can do this. I can ace this!"

"Don't treat your thoughts as facts unless there is real evidence to back them up.

Be tough with negativity and challenge it constantly.

FEAR can be False Evidence Appearing Real."

-- Lynne Namka

CHALLENGING IRRATIONAL FEARS

<u>Objective:</u> To distinguish between real fears and irrational ones and challenge irrational ones.

<u>Dialogue:</u> "Just when you thought it was safe, your greatest fear pops right out and says, 'Say Whaaat?' You and only you are the designer and developer of your life. You are in control of a large part of your destiny. But at times, you are held back by your fears.

Feelings of anxiety, fear and terror make us feel vulnerable and raw. Learning to manage unnecessary fear and calm yourself down is one of the most important things you can do to create a happy life. There are two kinds of fear: real and irrational. Real fears signal you to be wary and exercise caution. Real fears keep you safe and are needed for survival. It's helpful to be afraid of a burning hot stove or rattlesnakes. Irrational fears have no actual physical danger. Fear of failure, public speaking or performing are the more irrational kind of fears that pop up when you are not sure about yourself.

Too often we stay away from those things that frighten us. That gives the fear power and limits us. Many of our feelings have a hidden fear under them. Look for a hidden fear in feelings that are disturbing to you. What fears hide underneath your other feelings?

_____ Disappointment: Fear of not getting something that you wanted and feeling unhappy
_____ Anger: Fear of a goal being thwarted, being hurt or attacked, criticized or found guilty
_____ Awkward: Fear of feeling uncomfortable and not knowing what to say or do
_____ Anxiety: Fear of things going wrong and feeling out of control
_____ Sadness: Fear of loss of something or someone that helped you feel good
_____ Jealously: Fear of loss of the relationship and loss of feeling good about it.
_____ Insecurity: Fear of harm and not being emotionally or physically safe
_____ Insecurity: Fear of not being good enough or making a mistake
_____ Discouragement: Fear that the task is too hard or too much work
_____ Resentment: Fear that you will have to give up something you want
_____ Stubbornness: Fear that you will have to give up what you believe
_____ Despair: Fear that things will never get better or you'll never find meaning in life

So with irrational fears, the real Fear Factor is fear of feelings! We are afraid we can't handle something and the feelings that accompanying failure. Uncomfortable emotions are opportunities to learn more about yourself. Normal feelings and reactions can be processed and released.

<u>Activity:</u> Tame Your Fears. (Read Maurice Sendak's book, *Where the Wild Things, Are* to the children.) The best way to deal with fear is to face it. Look your fear of taking a test straight in the eye and tell it that it is not the boss of you and you will not allow it to shut you down. Confidence is something you create within yourself. How did Max tame those monsters that represented his fears? Did he give in to them? He danced with then and had a wild ruckus and said, "Be still! and tamed them with the magic trick of staring into their yellow eyes without blinking once..." How delightful it feels to master your fears.)

<u>Tips for parents and teachers:</u> An expanded version of this lesson is in my book Your Quick Anger Makeover. Teach your children Susan Jeffers' mantra from her book *'Feel your Fear and Do it Anyway!*

Expect more
of yourself
and you
will get more
of you

THE DYNAMICS OF DREAD: IF IT DOESN'T FEEL GOOD, DON'T DO IT!

Objective: To learn how the dynamics of dread and self doubt shut down becoming successful.

Dialogue: What do you hate to do the most and put off until you can't avoid anymore? Many of us have unproductive beliefs that cause you to put off dreaded tasks. Dread along with feelings of helplessness and discouragement come from doubting yourself. You will always doubt yourself until you use your Helper Words to finish the work. The more dread that you have the, less motivated you will be to get difficult tasks, complex projects and boring chores done. Too much dread creates a loser mentality.

Sometimes dread is rebellion against authority. Some part of you may be angry at a teacher or your parents so you refuse to do the work. Rebelling by putting off doing what you have to do can backfire on you. "You can't make me. Oh no! I can't even make me." Getting past rebelling is part of growing up.

Dread is one of those fear feelings that tries to shut you down. Not doing your job will cause you to feel bad about yourself and your self-esteem will drop. Tell yourself that you can push though negative thoughts and uncomfortable body tensions. After all, dread is just (1.) a feeling, (2.) negative ideas such as "I don't want to…" and (3.) body tension patterns.

Activity: Think of something you know how to do but don't want to do. Finish this sentence, "The thing(s) I avoid until the very last minute or never get around to doing is _____." Think about starting the project and watch what feelings and body tension comes up. Did your stomach become anxious? Did your hands or shoulders get tight? Did you get a slight headache and a drop in energy? These are the body sensations that go along with the feeling of dread. What did you tell yourself? Watch what you say to yourself to put off doing a job you must do. Catch yourself when you are being lazy. The more bad thoughts that you allow in your mind, the harder the work will be. Tell yourself, "For gosh sake, just get on with it. I'd better give myself a good talking to."

Giving into to feelings of dread will keep you from achieving your dreams. The longest walk will be getting up from the couch or bed and getting started if you give in to feelings of dread. When you find yourself doing a habit that you don't like, tell yourself, "Get a grip!" Give yourself a deep breath and a good talking to! Decide what kind of person you want to become and then decide what you will have to do to become this person. Challenge the unwillingness to start the task. Sometimes getting started is the hardest part. Decide to become a "Take Charge" person in your own life! Tell yourself that you will feel relief when you finish the job. You can turn on the feel-good endorphins in your brain's reward system by accomplishing the task. Remember to obtain your dream; you have to push that "Go Button."

Helper Words:
I can spend a lot of time hating the task, but I still have to do it.
I can dawdle and put it off, but I still have to do my work.
I refuse victim thinking. The best thing to do is to just get the job done.
Let's just start and see what happens. Just do it!

Tips for parents and teachers: Dread is one of those mind and body responses that keep us from achieving all we can. It is a major player emotion in people who procrastinate, are passive-aggressive or lazy. Unfortunately a larger number of young people have given in to a dread thinking habit. There is a peer culture of "Why try, it won't make a difference?" mentality which gives young people permission to avoid work. Empower your children by saying, "I'm proud of you for working so hard.

"Dread and procrastination are great time stealers. Don't be a foot dragger. Some things just need to be done. Just do it!"

-- Lynne Namka

AngriesOut.com
TimeToLoveYourself.com

DREAM STOPPERS AND COMMITTING TO GOING FOR WHAT YOU WANT

<u>Objective:</u> To identify future dreams and gain the motivation to go after them.

<u>Dialogue:</u> What are your dreams for a better you? What do you want to do with your life? Do you want to become a juicy human being? What is the one thing that has enough juice to carry you forward and make you work passionately? What are you excited about doing that you are willing to act on and make happen? Your Bucket List is the things you want to do before you get old. What do you want to do—travel, play professional sports, become a singer, become a lawyer, doctor, nurse or teacher, start your own company or have a happy family? What dreams do you want to put in your bucket?

Like the old philosopher said, "Know thyself." Know what "juices' you and what negative beliefs stop you dead in your tracks. Listen to this poem about putting off your dream by Langston Hughes:

"What happens to a dream deferred? Does it dry up like a raisin in the sun?
Or fester like a sore—and then run? Does it stink like rotten meat?
Or crust and sugar over—like syrupy sweet? Maybe it just sags like a heavy load.
Or does it explode?"

What will happen to you if you don't go after your dreams? Who will you become? Will you dry up like a raisin in the sun? Don't fail yourself. Let the real you stand up and get moving. The achieving, caring person is the real you. Dismiss the fake you who is cynical, depressed, lazy, helpless or angry. The fake you will cause you to lose your dreams by talking you out of them.

<u>Activity:</u> (Have the children write their answers to the Dream Stopper Worksheet.) If people try to stop you from doing your dream, tell them about Rudy. Are you willing to challenge your dream stopper beliefs? Keep your mind hopeful and your feet a moving in the right direction. Your dream is out there, go out and work for it. What can you tell yourself when you are hesitating doing something that is in your best interests to do?

<u>Helper Words:</u>
I'll be my own cheerleader and cheer myself as I go after my dream.
I stop telling myself excuses. Enough already.
Oh, get over yourself. Just get started. It's no big deal. What's the first step?
Onward and upward to start my dream by pushing that "Go Button!"

<u>Tips for parents and teachers:</u> Examine your own attitudes about how flexible you believe the mind is and what changes are possible with choosing a growth mindset. Do you really believe that people can change and grow if they give good effort? Michael Lerner said, "Energy always flows either toward hope, community, love, generosity, mutual recognition, and spiritual aliveness or it flows toward despair, cynicism, fear that there is not enough, paranoia about the intentions of others, and a desire to control and to turn everything in our reality into some-thing that can be controlled."

DREAM STOPPER WORKSHEET

You get to have dreams! What is your dream? What have you always wanted to do and knew you could but were afraid to risk?

_____

_____

Give a reason that you stop yourself from going after your dream. What are you afraid of—hard work, risking and failing, not following through, don't know where to start, etc?

_____

_____

What poor decision did you make that made you lose an old dream?

_____

_____

What small goal of moving towards your dream turned on pleasure chemicals in your brain?

_____

_____

What distractions are you going to have to ignore to get this goal? Video games, TV, other people?

_____

_____

If you could leave this world with one outstanding achievement, what would it be?

_____

_____

Whittle down what you no longer need. What bad habit would you have to give up to get the dream?

_____

_____

You will have to work hard. Are you willing to pay the costs for getting your dream? _____

If you achieve your dream, what is the best thing that might happen?

_____

_____

What kind of a person would you be if you did not have Dream Stopper beliefs in your mind?

_____

_____

What would your future look like if you change Dream Stopping beliefs?

_____

_____

BUT I'M BORED

Objective: To break into self-defeating beliefs about being bored.

Dialogue: If you want to put fear to work for you, be afraid, very afraid of becoming a bored, miserable person who doesn't find pleasure in life. You can learn a lot by watching people that you don't want to grow become. You see what they do that doesn't work and do the opposite. Let's list what people who are uninterested in things act like:

Dislike most things and downplay things that others like.
Have a cynical and negative attitude.
Moan, groan and complain.
Think of the worst thing that could happen and worry about it.
Have a chip on their shoulder and pick fights over imaginary slights.
Turn up the drama in social situations to feel alive.
Believe their life is set and predictable and they can't change.

Study people who are miserable most of the time and listen to them talk. Most people have a mix of healthy and unhealthy ways of thinking and acting. Look for the good in people and put those qualities for yourself. When they are negative, choose to do the opposite of what they say and do.
Words that you think and say are experienced deep in your brain and shape your life. Negative words can become habits that are at the center of your self esteem. You can actually give yourself a bad mood by telling yourself that you are bored. Words define you. Don't define yourself as a person who is bored—that is a sure fire way to become a boring person.

Activity: Words Make Up Who You Are. Notice your mood right now. On a scale from one to ten with one being not good and ten being the best, how do you feel right now? What number are you? Let's say together out loud, "I'm bored. There is nothing to do, I hate my life. It's useless, I'm bored." Watch how negative words drain your energy and pull you down. Did your posture change? Give yourself a number from one to ten now. How do you feel after pulling your energy with negativity? How did the energy in the room change? Now let's put in some positive words to shift your energy, Repeat after me, "I'm excited, I'm clever and creative, I'm unstoppable, I'm awesome, I'm in charge of putting positive words in my mind." Think of something that makes you feel pumped up and alive. What number from one to ten do you feel now? Look around and notice how everyone is different putting in the positive.

Take the "I'm bored" phrase out of your mind. If you feel yourself starting to feel bored, find something to do to interrupt being down in the dumps. Give new things a chance. Experiment and do new things you wouldn't ordinarily do. Keep searching and challenging any fixed, negative mindset. The trick is to be more in control of your own life. Choose the best from people you meet that you admire and become like them. Blow yourself away—say "Change starts here with me!"

Tips for parents and teachers: Some people have the idea that they must only do things that are enjoyable. I've worked with children as young as nine who refuse to do their homework because "It's boring" or "It's too much trouble or stupid," or "It's not fun, so I don't want to." They give up on learning and school due to fixed mindset beliefs. Recruiters recognize and dismiss young people joining the work force who don't have a good work ethic or a sense of responsibility and satisfaction for a job well done. Unfortunately some people have traded a pride in accomplishment for pride in getting out of work. Being proud of being lazy is a sure-fire set up for a loser life. We need to reinforce children for their effort and encourage them to reward themselves when they accomplish something.

 # Feeling bored? No big deal.

Bordeom is just an internal signal
to find something to do.

Refuse to be bored because that will
make you a boring person.

Boring work? So what?

There's nothing wrong with pushing
yourself through something tedious.

Make dull, boring work a challenge.

That builds character!"

ARE YOU AN EEYORE? GIVING MISERY A CHAIR TO SIT ON

Objective: To break into victim thinking.

Dialogue: Eeyore in Winnie the Pooh is that sad, little donkey that always sees the negative in everything. He looks for the possible thing and feels sorry for himself says, "Poor me. Bad things always happen to me!" Thinking about how bad you have it sets up a victim belief pattern that makes you depressed.

Activity: Eyore's Poor Self-esteem. Let's watch this video about Eeyore feeling bad about himself. http://www.youtube.com/watch?v=f_bD5SysAMk How does his attitude affect his having fun at the party? Don't buy into misery messages that aren't true about your being an unhappy person. Your mind is like a computer that you can program. Don't install a program that you are a victim.

Activity: (Read a chapter from *Winnie the Pooh* and contrast the personalities of Pooh who is happy about everything, Tigger, who jumps to new things restlessly seeking instant gratification and Eeyore who is fearful of trying new things and puts others down so he can feel better about himself. Milne's characters are metaphors for the different parts of ourselves. Point out the gloomy attitude and hang-down head of Eeyore and what he says to make himself miserable. Ask the children if they say misery messages or know adults who do.)

Activity: Off to the Misery Chair. A wise proverb goes "You can't keep misery from coming, but you don't have to give it a chair to sit on."To break your feeling sorry for yourself, give yourself a Misery Chair to sit on! Choose an uncomfortable chair such as a wooden chair. Put it in an out of the way place in your home that is dull and boring. If you are going to be miserable, might as well be as miserable as you can be!

Watch how your mind plays tricks on you to keep you in misery! Listen to yourself when you are in a bad mood and grouching about everything. Watch what your body does when you use negative words. Watch self-defeating words which limit you. Eeyore words are "I can't, never could, never will be able to...." I'm bored with...."

Change negative statements about yourself as lessons to be learned rather than absolute facts. The "I am ____ and that's it." "I am fat." could be changed to "Oops, waistband is too tight; time to cut back on the buttered popcorn." "I'm no good in Math." could be changed to "I've not done my Math homework lately or haven't taken the time to learn the multiplication tables." Say, "I made a mistake." rather than "I am bad, stupid, etc." If you start to feel sorry for yourself, take yourself off to the misery chair. Catch yourself in the act of becoming unhappy and give yourself a choice--either stop the negative thoughts at once or go sit in the misery chair. When you sit in the Misery Chair, be as miserable as you can be. Bring your unhappy thoughts to your full conscious mind. Go to it with a vengeance. Feel the physical discomfort of your body that matches the negative thoughts in your mind. How long do you want to be unhappy? Allow yourself a set time of five minutes of distress.

After making yourself good and miserable, cheer up and decide that you've had enough. Enough Eeyore, enough "Poor me. I shift my mind to the positive." Then go on about your business as usual. Clean up your life by cleaning up your negative thinking and language. Your words have power! Energy follows thought. You actually become what you think. Say and think only what you want to become.

Excuses! Excuses!

Fess up---

What keeps you from getting the job done?

It's hard for me and I hate doing hard stuff.

I find something more pleasurable to distract myself.

I don't do what I'm told to do because I need to rebel.

I don't like the bad feelings that doing hard work brings.

I feel bored and I can't stand that feeling.

I put it off until the last minute so the pressure
of the deadline motivates me to act.

I don't want to do things that make me feel stupid.

MOTIVATION: TAKE YOUR PLAN TO ACTION

<u>Objective:</u> To learn to break into procrastination thoughts.

<u>Dialogue:</u> Dreams are just good ideas that you fantasize about unless you act on them to make them happen. Making a dream come true involves taking risks and hard work. It is too easy to put things off that we don't want to do. Putting things off that need to be done is called procrastination. We procrastinate when the task is hard and we feel uncomfortable inside. We distract ourselves with more pleasurable activities to feel good. We drag our feet and put off what doesn't feel good and then, oh no, nothing gets done! We create little white lies as we wait for the right mood to motivate us. But deep down we know they are excuses.

Procrastination is the big thief of time. Not taking action at the right time and not following through on something you care about steals from your dream. As a wise woman said, "Work as hard as you can, imagine immensities, don't compromise, and don't waste time. Start now. Not twenty years from now, not two weeks from now. Now!"

<u>Activity:</u> Do you play procrastination tricks with your mind? Do you tell yourselves, 'I don't feel like doing this now? I'll feel more like it tomorrow." Think about it. What do you put off and give into the distractions that undermine your work? Make a list of the excuses you say to sabotage your own success.

http://www.youtube.com/watch?v=uqGz7uqoPZ4

Watch this video of the many excuses you can give yourself. Sound familiar? Get over it! Just do it! Just gear up and get ready. http://www.youtube.com/watch?v=mEHQ9tzJpYA

<u>Activity:</u>   Words have power. Your negative words sour your mood. Fixed mindset excuses such as "I can't do it. It's too hard. It's too much trouble," are victim thinking which will give you a miserable life. Complete the Why Should I Change? worksheet. Being aware that you have a problem is the first step to change. Imagine yourself doing the task and succeeding.

<u>Helper Words:</u>
I'm telling myself procrastination words again. Cut it out!
 I stop putting energy into pooh-poohing myself and get busy.
I challenge myself to walk through the fear of change.
Dreams come true when I'm willing to work at them.

<u>Tips for parents and teachers:</u> Never call your child lazy as that might lead to a self-fulfilling prophesy. Set up the hope for change in an unmotivated child by telling him or her that someday they will find their passion and that important find will lead to something great. Apps to deal with procrastination can be found at http://www.edudemic.com/procrastination-tools/.

Don't Let Putting Things Off Rule You!

It's what you do every day that counts.

Do the work so it is out of your way!

Stuff not done nags, nags and nags at you.

Beat it to the punch and dismiss the nag.

Challenge that procrastination demon who says,
"Later. You can do it later."

Don't wait to get in the mood.

Do it if you don't feel like it.

Do it especially if you don't feel like it."

Day by day, you stretch your smarts.

Celebrate that simple phrase, "Get 'er done."

Getting work done gives you freedom!

CHOOSING THE BEST FROM YOUR FAMILY

<u>Objective</u>: To give permission to choose from helpful family behaviors and learn from positive outside influences.

<u>Activity</u>: Notice how some people in your family deal with setbacks and things going wrong. Some have the skills to take things in stride while others might think they are beaten down and become a victim. Some family members become worried or depressed. Some buckle down and try harder. Think of someone in your family or someone you know who handles stress well. Who gives up easily or who seems to cause more problems for themselves and others? Some young people live in families where people are supportive but in other families the grownups are angry, fight a lot or misuse alcohol or drugs.

Some boys and girls are wiser than their parents. They know they are different from some of the unhappy people in their family. They notice what doesn't work and look for more productive ways than what their family does. They read books to find out how happy families treat each other. They find other people outside their family to support them. They go on to become good students, athletes or singers and develop talents and skills. They love their families but they seek a sense of belonging to something positive outside their unhappy families.

Poet Maya Angelou said, "Do the best that you can do until you know better. Then when you know better, do better." What does this mean? Give an example of when you did something wrong because you didn't know better and then you learned and changed your behavior.

You can choose the best ways of coping from your family and let the rest go! Stop and think. What does someone in your family do that you don't want to do when you grow up? Take the best your parents have to teach you and keep adding more positive ways of thinking and acting. If you can't figure out a problem, get advice from someone who handles things well. Break away from the "I can't" mindset and challenge yourself to keep looking for a solution. Let challenge change you!

<u>Helper Words</u>
I choose the best things my family does and let the rest go.
Anything is possible if I've got the courage to get 'er done.
I choose friends who bring out the best in me rather than the stress in me.
I challenge stress rather than letting it challenge me.

<u>Tips for parents and teachers</u>: Children deal with all types of tough problems. What do you say to a six-year-old boy who is numb because his father tried to kill himself the night before? I was called in at our school for children with emotional and behavioral disorders to talk with him. I expressed sorrow and said I hoped his dad would get better. I told him that I knew he loved his dad and that there were many things his dad did that he liked. I suggested that he could be like his dad in what worked but not in the ways that didn't work. In our school, he had learned about healthy ways to act and he could choose the best ways for himself. He wasn't ready to talk about his feelings about his dad's suicide attempt so we went off to throw a basketball against the gym wall.

Resilient Young People are Flexible!

They do the positive things that the members of their family do.

They stop doing things that the people in their family do that don't work.

They decide to make something of them by becoming go-getters.

They challenge fixed mindset thoughts and negative thinking.

They study hard and feel proud that they are problem solvers.

They understand that success is learning from making mistakes.

They read about how other people got out of unhappy situations.

They make friends with caring people who encourage them.

They give self praise after finishing small goals.

They ignore distractions of others who take them away from their goal.

They minimize fun activities like video games that take them off track.

The better they feel about working hard, the easier it is to do more!

FINDING A MENTOR

Objective: To gain support from trusting people during times of crisis.

Dialogue: No one needs to go it alone. We all need social support. When things are really rough, you can reach out and find someone to be in your corner. (Write Success Mentor and a ☺ on the board.) A mentor can be an older person who supports you and believes in you. A success mentor is someone who can give you advice or help you deal with problems. Spending time around a caring person can bring you back to a happier mood. It's good to have someone in your corner that you can talk to when you have a problem. A problem shared is a problem halved. You deserve to have someone be there for you.

Activity: When the dark storm clouds start to roll in who could help you weather the storm? Look around to see who might mentor you. Stop and think about who are good problem solvers and have a good head on their shoulders. Who is the wisest person you know? Choose people you admire who have good values to help you know right from wrong. During rough times, people fall into three categories of leavers, stayers who make things worse and problems solvers:

(1.) Leavers. Some people withdraw or disappear at the first sign of trouble.
(2.) Stormers: Those who stick around to make things worse. Watch out for the people who turn up the drama.
(3.) Problem solvers who give you support.

Discussion Questions
Who tries to tell you that you can't make something of yourself?
Who puts you down because they are afraid you will succeed?
Who in your family or neighborhood looks out for you?
Who is there for you if you need help? Who has your back?
Who would help you get a new outlook on this issue?
 Who is the wisest, kindest person you know that you could ask to help you?

Activity: Asking for help. This video features Steve Jobs who developed the Apple computer, Ipad and Ipod talking about his asking for help with a project when he was twelve years old. He also reminds us that being willing to fail and try again is part of getting the project done.
http://www.youtube.com/watch?v=zkTf0LmDqKI

Give yourself permission to ask several people to be your mentor or your "just-a-little-bit mentor" (put your index finger and thumb apart to show just a little bit.) You may have to explain what a mentor is to them by saying "I need someone to be in my corner. Could you give me a "heads up" when I need it? Would you notice if I'm going in the wrong direction and give me feedback? Could you talk with me about what it means to be successful?"

Not everyone you ask will want to be your mentor and might say no to you. That's okay as they might not have the time or have too many problems of their own. Keep trying if the first or second person doesn't have time. Be willing to take advice from your mentor. Listen to what they say and decide for yourself if it is in your best interests or not. Take their good ideas and discard what doesn't work for you. Give your mentor appreciation and support back. Let them know that you appreciate their being in your life. Adults need to know that their efforts are appreciated.

Mentors

If you find someone who
looks out for you,
checks up on you and
is kind, don't let them go.
They are a true friend
People like that are
hard to find.

©dianne j. hook

LESSONS FROM RUDY

<u>Objective:</u> To learn to keep goals and not let others talk you out of them.

<u>Dialogue:</u> It's good to have a dream of what you want for your life. Your dream may change as you grow older but that is okay. You may not get the exact dream that you want but by going towards it, you will get other good things. The old dream may change but new and exciting ones will come in if you put your mind on what you want and go after it.

<u>Activity:</u> Rudy: A Tribute. Let's watch Rudy as a little boy being laughed at by his family about his dream of going to Notre Dame to play football. They laughed at him because he wasn't that smart and was 5 foot seven inches tall and weighed only 160 pounds which is small for a football player.

http://www.youtube.com/watch?v=RSqAOzJu7Mg

In this video, Rudy was told by his dad that he couldn't achieve his dream.

http://www.youtube.com/watch?v=QsmzDL61oME

<u>Dialogue:</u> Have other people tried to talk you out of some exciting dream for your life? Some people will encourage you and cheer you on. Others will try to stop you and pooh pooh your dream. Some will try to distract you by dangling risky ideas before you. Some people don't want others to be successful. Stop and think. Tell us what others have said to discourage you and we'll write them on the board so you can challenge any fixed mindset beliefs. Remember fixed mindset beliefs are always self-limiting and we don't want you to limit yourself in any way. Find people who support you. Be strong enough to know what you stand for. Be brave enough to ask for it. Be smart enough to know when you need someone in your corner. Courage is reaching out for help when you need it.

This video shows Rudy's coach telling him not to quit and give his very best and other motivational clips from different movies. http://www.youtube.com/watch?v=MYKsbld6LII

See Rudy making the big play as his dream comes true.
http://www.youtube.com/watch?v=mZ7ZpLgkVxA

Remember Rudy, the small boy who kept telling himself that he could get his dream of being a football player at Notre Dame? Here's a video of the real Rudy talking about his problems of paying attention in class as he had a learning disorder.
Part 1: http://www.youtube.com/watch?v=vEGOTWwd14M

Set Small Goals. The real Rudy discussing setting small goals and working hard to move closer to his big goal of running out of the tunnel with the Notre Dame football team.
http://www.youtube.com/watch?v=VL4fEUKwdPw

<u>Give Yourself Permission Words to Find a Mentor</u>
I find people who can look out for my best interests.
I deserve to get some positive input from people I trust.
 I'm open to feedback and a different way of looking at a problem.
If I really want something, I go after it.

Put your mind on what you care about and go after it.

Jump in and take the plunge right through

uncertainty and uncomfortable feelings. Dreams
are made by action and getting one "small win"
after another until they add up to "BIG WINS."

You make your own opportunities though daily habits
that take you towards your goal.

Your choices and actions actively
create who you become!

150

GIVERS AND TAKERS

<u>Objective:</u> To raise consciousness about being fair and giving and receiving one's fair share.

<u>Dialogue:</u> In this world, there are people who give too much and those who take too much. Have you noticed that some people think only of themselves? Some children ask others for too much. Others never feel free to ask for what they want; they give themselves away.

All human behaviors can be put on a line from too much of a behavior to too little of it. (Draw a long line across the board. Put the "Takers" with the words "Me, Me, Me" on one far end and "Givers" with the words, "I give myself away." Add the words "Just Right—giving and receiving" in the middle range of the line.) People who are the happiest are here in the middle which is the balance between giving and receiving from others. So it's tricky to get the balance—you can ask for what you want but you don't want to take too much.

It's okay to want new things but it's not okay to take more than your share or to keep begging people for what you want. It is not okay to be happy about getting something at the expense of someone else. Takers are more focused on getting things—they want material objects. When you get something new you might get a short burst of pleasure but it doesn't last. People adapt to the pleasure of things that cost money but the good feeling quickly wears off. You get excited about new toys at Christmas but you forget about them quickly. Things do not make you happy. Happiness is an inside job. Happiness does not come from being popular. It comes from being connected with people you care about.

<u>Activity:</u> Think of someone who is selfish. Don't say who it is; just think about this person. Come to the board and draw a stick figure where you think he or she might fall on this line. Now think about someone who is too generous and does not think of themselves. Draw a stick figure where you think they might fall on this line. Think of someone in the "Just Right' range where they are giving and loving but allow others to give back to them. Where do they fall on this line? Think about where you might be on this line. Where are you on this line? Watch how much you expect things from other people or how you give up your needs to meet theirs. Where would you like to be on the line? Are you willing to change?

People do not become happy by getting things. Family and friends who are there for you and you are there for them create true happiness. The stronger friendships you have with others, the better. Having a faith with a belief in something bigger than yourself creates happiness. Having goals that are meaningful to work on which uses your strengths and abilities also make for lifelong happiness.

<u>Helper Words</u>
I surround myself with people who support me.
I look for things that truly make me happy not just new things
I catch myself when I beg and am too demanding from my parents.
I support others. I'm a kind of person who is there for people.
I balance my life with being between giving and receiving from others.

<u>Tips for parents and teachers:</u> Materialism has negative direct effects on a person's well-being and makes bad events even worse. Dealing with negative events by going shopping is a poor coping defense. Highly materialistic individuals had more impulsive buying than their less-materialistic peers. They had a higher level of distress and tougher time recovering from setbacks and higher levels of post-traumatic stress.

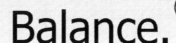

Balance.

Most things in life
are about balance.

Do the right amount,
not too little and
not too much.

Follow the Goldilocks
Principal of getting to the
"Ahhh, just right!"

©dianne j. hook

YOU DON'T ALWAYS GET WHAT YOU WANT

<u>Objective:</u> To learn to accept the word "No" for an answer.

<u>Dialogue:</u> Some people get angry when they don't get what they ask. Some children become angry when they are asked to pick up their toys, to go to bed, or being refused a toy at the store. They create problems for themselves by believing they should get something just because they wanted it. They will be much happier in life if they can learn to hear and accept the word "No."

Life is full of yeses and nos. Learning to handle the feelings of disappointment when a goal is thwarted is a major skill in life. Feeling disappointed can make you feel desperate inside. Some people fall apart when told no and either give up feeling hopeless or angry. Some get angry and have a tantrum. Some keep on insisting that they be given what they want. This is called nagging or badgering. Some children badger their parents into giving in.

One very important skill in growing up is learning to handle disappointment. Is it a good idea to make yourself unhappy by getting angry when you don't get your way? Name your feeling of disappointment and tell yourself that you are disappointed but you can handle it. Tell yourself, "I take what I get and I don't throw a fit!" Remember what Cookie Monster said, "Me want it but me wait."

<u>Activity:</u> (Have the children role play handling disappointment over not getting to go to an event or get a toy at the store. Cast yourself in the role of not getting your way and throwing a tantrum in the first skit to show the children how immature it can look.)

Feelings of disappointment are normal when things don't go your way. It is what you do with them that count. Challenge that outburst of frustration that you have when things don't go the way you want. If you start to act out the frustration, catch yourself and choose a Helper Word statement to calm yourself down. You can own your mistakes, problems and feelings and feel good about yourself.

<u>Helper Words:</u>
I didn't get what I wanted this time. Oh, well; that's life.
Sometimes I get what I want; sometimes I don't. That's just how it is.
It's my parent's job to say no some of the time. I handle not getting what I want.
Even though I don't like to hear no, disappointment is just a feeling that I can handle.

<u>Tips for parents and teachers:</u> Today's children are more entitled than any other generation. Not being able to handle disappointment and to keep on pushing to get what one wants at the expense of others is a precursor to narcissism. Narcissistic people are able ignore distractions and hone their focus to keep on hammering the person to get their way. (Think of an obnoxious telemarketer who keeps insisting after you say no.) Business people know that negotiations are still open as long as people stay at the table talking about a deal. They know that they have to walk away when a relentless negotiator won't take no for an answer! Use this walking away strategy with a firm
No! I said no!" and make yourself unavailable.

SOMETIMES I GET WHAT I WANT. SOMETIMES I DON'T.

THE GOLDILOCKS PRINCIPLE: AHH—JUST RIGHT

Objective: To understand the underlying dynamics of narcissistic and codependency thinking.

Dialogue: Remember the story of Goldilocks and the Three Bears? In the fairy tale, what did Goldilocks say when she tasted the porridge? She said, "This porridge is too hot. This porridge is too cold. This porridge is just right! This chair is too hard. This chair is too soft. This chair is just right." The Goldilocks Principle applied to people is too much or too little of any behavior or emotion causes imbalance. The Goldilocks Principle says that too much or too little of anything can become out of balance.

Goldilocks' Just Right Principle

Ahhh--Just Right!

→		←
I expect others to give to me..	I give and receive equally.	I must give too much away.
I get my way most of the time.	I take turns and share.	I rarely get my way.
I demand to get what I want.	I ask politely for what I want.	I can't ask for what I want.

This chart is adapted from my book, Your Quick Anger Makeover

Have you ever helped someone so much that you felt taken advantage of? Givers have not learned to say 'No" so others walk all over them. If you give too much, you give yourself away and feel drained. If you give too much, you might burn out. People experience burnout when they use up too much of their resources and then feel resentful and angry. They have not learned to say no and set boundaries when others ask for too much. Givers have to set boundaries because takers don't.

Takers want their way most of the time and believe that their needs are more important than others. Are you the kind of person who can talk others into giving you what you want? You may feel good about getting things but you won't end up with deep and true friends. If you have been told that you are spoiled and get your way more than others, you might want to look at this part of your personality. It is not who you are. It's something that you have learned and you can unlearn it.

If you take too much or give too much, you can move over into the "Ahhh, Just Right" place here in the middle. Just Right people balance give and take. They think about both themselves and others. They recognize those people who are self-centered and don't notice the needs of others. The happiest people are just right; they know it is okay to do both giving and receiving. They value themselves and they value others. They are quick to help others in a team sport. They don't worry about who gets credit. They put the needs of the team ahead of their own. Just Right people are generous with others and they allow others to give them things as well. Because they are open minded and friendly, people are friendly back. Others are there to help them when they need it.

Activity: Decide Who You Want to be Like. Who are the selfish people in your neighborhood? Who are the givers and takers in your church? Who do you like better—givers or takers? Are you an "Ask too much from others" or a "Don't ask enough" type of person. Good friendships are about each person getting some of their needs met some of the time. You have the power to decide what type of person you want to be. .

TRUE FRIENDS:

Are kind to you.

Have your back.

Stick up for you.

Make you feel good about yourself.

Are happy to share with you.

Are fun to be with.

Are not mean to you.

Cheer you up when you are down.

Don't make you feel bad about who you are.

Don't get you in trouble.

CREATING A PEACEFUL WORLD

<u>Objective</u>: To give the idea that each one of us has a part in bringing peace to our small part of the world.

<u>Dialogue</u>: You young people are the wave of the future. You will have a hand in determining what type of world you live in. What kind of classroom do you want to have? When you grow up, what type of family do you want to have? When those who take more than their share become better givers, the world will be friendlier and we will have more peace. Put yourself in the Goldilocks Zone—not too hot and not too cold. Not too much taking and not too much giving. What kind of world do you want to live in? Ahhh, just right!

<u>Activity</u>: Song A Random Act of Kindness. http://www.youtube.com/watch?v=SaHFj_68cKs . Elijah the Superhero - A children's video about random acts of kindness http://www.youtube.com/watch?v=SQ7m_0NYgFE Pay happiness forward. The motto is if you give a little love, you can get a bit of your own. Discuss what the children have done to surprise others with kindness. Do you make a point to notice when someone needs your help? What random acts of kindness have you done lately?

<u>Activity</u>: Empty Stuff versus Important Stuff. Do you spend too much time filling your head with empty stuff like celebrity gossip, excessive fashion, excessive sports statistics and video games? These things are fun to follow and know about but if you focus on them too much, you might miss out on some other important things. Moderation of the things that don't mean much with doing things that make a difference is the best policy.

<u>Activity</u>: Peace Dude. Read some of Robert Silverstein's *People for Peace* children's stories about Peace Dude and other online children's stories at http://www.peacekids.net/stories/index.htm.

<u>Tips for parents and teachers:</u> Children need coaching on how to make and keep friends. One of the best books on how to make and keep friends is the old classic Dale Carnegie's *How to Make Friends and Influence People*. As Carnegie notes it is amazing how much a smile can affect others and how a genuine interest in other people can make them feel important. My writings on narcissism are listed on my website *Get Your Nardar On* at http://www.nardar.com. If everyone could learn to recognize and counteract extreme selfish behavior, we would have less of it in the world. See my article on Checks and Balances.

MAKING AND GIVING WARM FUZZIES

<u>Objective</u>: To learn that happiness happens when helping others.

<u>Materials</u>: Chenille balls cut from trim for curtains or plain cotton balls and stick-on plastic eyes.

<u>Dialogue</u>: Think of a happy person that you know. What is a Signature Strength that they have? Are they a giving person who enjoys helping others? Do good things and good things will come your way. One secret to success is to help others succeed. That's right. You can become a successful human being by doing good. Here is a double winner idea: feel good about yourself for helping someone else.

What do you do when you see someone who is upset? Do you ask them what is wrong or try to help them? You can show that you are a caring person when you notice someone who is sad or hurt.

Did anyone find a mentor they could tell us about? What did you learn from your mentor? Become a mentor yourself to the smaller children. Friendly faces mean a lot to younger children when they are having a hard time. When you see someone in need of support, remember when you felt down and someone was there for you. Step up and cheer them on and encourage them to do their best. You don't have to take them on as a best friend, just offer a small bit of your time. It could make all the world of difference to someone who is down on themselves.

<u>Activity</u>: To Be a Good Friend. The way to have a friend is to be friendly and befriend someone. There are young people who need your special acts of kindness. Look around on the playground or neighborhood for someone who could benefit from your smile or a happy word. Here are some ideas about befriending someone else. Give some examples of when you did some of these things with a friend. Now think about recess and which one you would like to practice.

To Be a Good Friend

Show interest in what the person likes.
Find fun things that you have in common.
Feel good about making the person feel good.
Notice and appreciate your friend's feelings.
Avoid arguments and aggressive behavior.

Have fun conversations.
Listen to what the person has to say.
Feel good about taking turns.
Ignore small negative behaviors.

<u>Activity</u>: Making Warm Fuzzies. Warm Fuzzies are written words of encouragement that you write down with a smiley face ☺ picture. Let's make some Warm Fuzzies from the balls and eyes. Think of someone at home who would feel good about getting a note from you saying you appreciate what they do or who they are. Write a positive note about what you like about them. They can pass your Warm Fuzzy on to someone else. (Make some Warm Fuzzy notes yourself to pass on to the children and other teachers or family members.)

<u>Helper Words</u>:
I'll be a Resilience Coach and encourage others to do their best.
I don't have to fix someone else's problems. I am just there for them.
I'll look around for someone who needs encouragement.
I'll give them a Warm Fuzzy and remind them to give themselves one too.

Respect is earned not given.

When you respect yourself, others respect you.

No matter what people have said about you,
it's how you think about yourself that matters.

You have control over how you present yourself.

Stand tall.

Show that you are a person worthy of respect.

©dianne j. hook

BECOMING A ROLE MODEL FOR OTHERS

<u>Objective:</u> To learn that helping others is associated with good self-esteem.

<u>Discussion:</u> Loving, generous people are role models for how each of us can choose to live our lives. Kind people have learned a special secret that it feels good to be giving. When they care about other people, they feel good themselves. It's a win-win situation.

<u>Activity:</u> Who is the most loving and kind person you know? Tell us who you admire for their ability to make others feel good? How do you feel around that person? How do they treat you? What do they do that makes you feel good about yourself? What have you learned from being around this person? How have you become a better person by just watching how they act? How are you like this person you admire? Make yourself proud. Notice other kids who are having a difficult time. Make yourself into a friendly person that others respect and like. Being kind helps you develop a good character and make many friends. Be kind to each other even if you disagree on stuff. Be kind even if the person is not someone you hang out with.

Some of our greatest heroes have come from a tough background and unhappy families. In growing up they made mistakes like everyone does. They learned that when the going gets tough, the tough get going. They set long-term goals and then did what it took to attain them. They broke the goals into doable steps and worked right through them. Heroes learn early to see setbacks as lessons that make then stronger. They worked to make their minds flexible and positive so they could push themselves through when things are hard.

Think of those who need your special words of encouragement. Be willing to help those people who have special needs. If you have the power to make someone happy, why not do it? If you have something that someone needs and you can spare it, why not share it? Make both of you happy in one action. You can be a hero and help others when they need it. What defines a hero? Heroes see what needs to be done and step up and do it. Who is your favorite hero who is a real live person or one from history? Tell us what this person did that was heroic.

<u>Helper Words</u>
I can be someone positive for someone who needs it.
I'll be a role model of giving to others.
I can be a hero giving of myself to others.
I can offer support when one of my friends or family members is down.

<u>Tips for parents and teachers:</u> Character counts. Look for opportunities to praise your children for making the hard choices that promote good character. Tell the children often that you believe in them and their ability to put forth good effort, complete hard work and deal with challenges. See and comment on the best in them so they can see the best in themselves. *Random Acts of Kindness* is a book and a movement that helps create a kinder world. See http://www.randomactsofkindness.org/ for free and creative ways to encourage children to help others. *Kids' Random Acts of Kindness* by Conari Press and *Ordinary Mary's Extraordinary Deed* by Emily Pearson are two books about helping others

Clip art © www.djinkers.com

WEAR YOUR POSITIVE CAPS

<u>Objective:</u> To reinforce cooperation, problem solving, sharing and affirming others.

<u>Materials:</u> Paper, crayons or markers, glitter or other small decorative materials.

<u>Activity:</u> I Put on My Thinking CAPS. Minds are a wonderful thing when you learn to make them to be positive. You can create a happier classroom or family by learning four important skills of cooperating, problem solving, sharing and affirming others. (Discuss the four concepts with the children. Have them fold paper caps from large sheets of Manila or newsprint paper. Have each child make four caps and designate these as their Thinking CAPS. Decorate each cap and label them with the different skills☺)

C--Cooperation Cap. Discuss how children in the family or class can share and cooperate with each other. Have them draw pictures on the Cooperation Cap while they practice cooperating with each other.

A--Affirmation Cap. Affirmations are positive things that we say about others and ourselves. Have the children draw Warm Fuzzies on their Affirmation Caps.

P--Problem Solving Cap. Have the children write their favorite problem solver Helper Words on their caps.

S--Sharing Feelings Cap. Have the children write the names of and draw pictures of the different feelings on this cap.

<u>Dialogue:</u> A lack of resources can cause conflict. What can we do when there is not enough pie to go around? Generate as many alternatives as possible. One answer that is often overlooked is to bake a bigger pie! Set up a problem, which could be solved through cooperation such as having too few crayons at the table. Have the children give examples of positive experiences of working together cooperatively.

<u>Teacher Cues:</u>
Stop and think. Do you need to put on one of your CAPS? Which one?
Put on your Sharing Feelings Cap and tell us how you felt last weekend.
This group seems to be having a problem. Put on your Cooperation Cap and figure it out.
I feel good when I see the members of this group are all wearing their Cooperation Caps!

<u>Helper Words for Children:</u>
Let's all put on our Cooperation Caps while we work together.
I'd like to talk to you. I'll put on my Sharing Feelings Cap.
I feel good about remembering to put on one or more of my caps.
We are the fourth graders (or the Smith family.) We do things together.

<u>Tips for parents and teachers:</u> Working on classroom units help children feel good about being connected to the group when positive social skills are encouraged. Skills such as listening and working together on projects of mutual interest are generated in unit or family projects.

Boost Your Self Esteem

Make the right decisions, not the easy ones.

How you feel about yourself affects
everything you say and do.

Use Happy Helper Words to shift your mood.

Throw out those old "defeat-yourself" words.

When you feel positive about yourself,
your future is optimistic.

Shift your gears into the Positive!

Give yourself permission to feel gooooood!

MAKING A YOU TUBE VIDEO ON RESILIENCE

<u>Objective:</u> To put learning into practice by teaching others about resilience.

<u>Activity:</u> Making a You Tube Video. (Do a cooperative project of making a video for other children. Choose a director, script writers, graphic designer for the title and end page, camera people and actors. Have a committee that gets permission from the school principal, school board. Choose another committee to contact the various television, newspaper and radio media for publicity. Discuss what social media could be used to further publicize the video.

Have the entire group develop the direction and theme of the video, who their target audience is and the goals they want to achieve. Film different children talking about what resilience means to them, setbacks they bounced back from, skills and tools they used to deal with bad times, what Helper Words they use to remind themselves that they are strong, etc.

You and the children could develop other videos of Becoming a Happy Person, Developing a Successful Life or It's Okay to Make Mistakes as Long as You Learn from Them.)

You may use any of the posters from this book in the video as fillers for the video. Please give credit to *Lesson Plans for Teaching Resilience to Children* by Lynne Namka and http://www. angriesout.com at the credits at the end. This will link your video to my other You Tube and other web projects of antibullying, anger management and teaching emotional intelligence to children.

If you email me at lnamka158@earthlink.net and let me know, I'll publicize your video on my Facebook page and my Inspiration and Transformation newsletter which goes out weekly to 4000 people worldwide.

To Become Truly Happy

..act as you would like to become.

..challenge negative thoughts with Thought Stoppage.

..get a balance of good work and play.

..choose good books, music and interesting hobbies.

..have an open mind about your ability to change.

..feel good about learning new things.

..take responsibility for mistakes and clean them up.

..stand tall and put a smile on your face.

..surround yourself with happy people.

..choose friends who treat you well.

..know and develop your Signature Strengths.

..find meaning and develop a purpose-filled life.

..be gentle and loving with yourself and others.

Web Resources

Dr. Carol Dweck discusses How to Talk about Success and Failure Effectively at http://www.youtube.com/watch?v=sM65R78gzPY

You can take part in a web-based research project about the behaviors that make you happy with tests from Dr. Martin Seligman and his colleagues at www.authentichappiness.org.

The Penn Resiliency Project Martin Seligman and Co-Directors: Jane Gillham, Ph.D. & Karen Reivich, Ph.D. http://www.ppc.sas.upenn.edu/prpsum.htm or http://www.reachinginreachingout.com/programs-bb&t.htm.

Brainology® is a curriculum with videos for teachers developed by Carol Dweck and her colleagues. There are teacher versions in English and in Spanish (Brainology Español). Brainology® is on You Tube http://www.youtube.com/watch?v=pF5yB31IT5Y

Families OverComing Under Stress (FOCUS) is a resiliency training program of six to eight sessions for families with preschoolers and up and couples facing adversity and traumatic stress. Education is given on child development, impact of stress on families, post traumatic stress disorder and problem-solving communication skills. http://nfrc.ucla.edu/

HomeFront Strong is an eight week resiliency group for military spouses or partners experiencing distress associated with deployment that helps build social support and positive relationships and promote resiliency and positive coping. http://m-span.org/programs-for-military-families/homefront-strong/

The American Psychological Association provides a *Roads to Resilience Brochure* explaining that the primary factor in resilience is having caring and supportive relationships within and outside the family that create love and trust, provide role models and give support. http://www.apa.org/helpcenter/road-resilience.aspx.

The STRoNG Military Families is a ten-week parenting program for military service members, partners, and children 1-to-6 years old designed to support and enhance the resilience of military families. http://m-span.org/programs-for-military-families/strong-families/

The Mindset Works® SchoolKit is at http://www.youtube.com/watch?v=rtybeteZNDg

My blog for parents is at http://timetoloveyourself.com/blog/how-to-talk-with-a-kid-with-a-bad-attitude/

Think Positive to Stay Positive: http://www.scribd.com/doc/36845603/Think-Positive-to-Stay-Positive-Teaching-Children-the-Benefits-of-Using-Positive-Self-Sentences.

Clip Art http://www.djinkers.com/home.php

References

Carney, D. R.; Cuddy, A. J.; and Yap, A. (2010). "Power Posing– Brief Nonverbal Displays Affect Neuroendocrine Levels and Risk Tolerance". *Journal of the Association for Psychological Science.*

Dweck, C. S. (1999). *Self-theories: Their role in motivation, personality and development.* Philadelphia: Taylor and Francis/Psychology Press.

Dweck, C. S. (2006). *Mindset: The new psychology of success.* New York: Random House.

Faber, A., and Mazlish, E. (2012). *How to talk so kids will listen and listen so kids will talk.* New York: Scribner Books.

Grant, H., & Dweck, C. S. (2003). Clarifying achievement goals and their impact. *Journal of Personality and Social Psychology.*

Ginsburg, K. R. (2011). *Building resilience in children and teens: Giving kids roots and wings.* Washington, D.C.: American Academy of Pediatrics.

Halvorson, H. and Dweck, C. (2011). *Succeed: How we can reach our goals.* New York: Plume.

Kamins, M., and Dweck, C. S. (1999). Person vs. process praise and criticism: Implications for contingent self-worth and coping. *Developmental Psychology.*

Hoff, B. (1992). *The Tao of Piglet.* New York: Penguin Books.

Lieberman, M. D., Eisenberger, N. I., Crockett, M. J., Tom, S. M., Pfeifer, J. H. Way, B. M.(2007). Putting feelings into words: affect labeling disrupts amygdala activity in response to affective stimuli. *Psychological Science.*

Masten, C. L., Eisenberger, N. I., Borofsky, L. A. Pfeifer, J. H. (2009). Social cognitive and affective neural correlates of social exclusion during adolescence: Understanding the distress of peer rejection. *Neuroscience.*

Mueller, C. M., & Dweck, C. S. (1998). Intelligence praise can undermine motivation and performance. *Journal of Personality and Social Psychology.*

Nussbaum, A. D., & Dweck, C. S. (2007). Defensiveness vs. remediation: Self-theories and modes of self-esteem maintenance. *Personality and Social Psychology Bulletin.*

Peterson, C., Park, N., & Seligman, M. E. P. (2005). Assessment of character strengths. In G. P. Koocher, J. C. Norcross, & S. S. Hill III (Eds.), *Psychologists' desk reference.* New York: Oxford University Press.

Peterson, C., Park, N., & Seligman, M. E. (2005). Orientations to happiness and life satisfaction: The full life versus the empty life. *Journal of Happiness Studies.*

Peterson, C., & Seligman, M. E. P. (2004). *Character strengths and virtues: A handbook and classification.* Washington, D.C.: American Psychological Association.

Reivich, K., and Shatte, A. (2003). *The resilience factor: 7 keys to finding your inner strength and overcoming life's hurdles.* New York: Harmony Books.

Riera, M. (2003). *Staying connected to your teenager: How to keep them talking to you and how to hear what they're really saying.* Cambridge, MA: Da Capo Press.

Salmansohn. K., (2008). *The bounce back book: How to thrive in the face of adversity, setbacks, and losses.* New York: Workman Publishing Company, Inc.

Siebert, A., (2005). *The resiliency advantage: Master change, thrive under pressure, and bounce back from setbacks.* San Francisco: Berrett-Koehler Publishers.

Seligman, M. (2007). *The optimistic child: A proven program to safeguard children against depression and build lifelong resilience.* New York: Mariner Books.

Seligman, M. (2012). *Flourish: A visionary new understanding of happiness and well-being.* New York: Atria Books.

Seligman, M., Reivich, K., Jaycox, L., and Gillham, J. (1995). *The optimistic child: A revolutionary approach to raising resilient children.* Boston: Houghton Mifflin.

Tough, P. *How children succeed: grit, curiosity and the hidden power or character.* (2013). Mariner Books.

Talk, Trust and Feel Therapeutics

Talk, Trust & Feel Therapeutics provides innovative toys and books to help parents, teachers and therapists teach children to express uncomfortable feelings, take responsibility for their own behavior and learn positive social skills. Our commitment is to develop products to help children feel good about identifying and breaking into their acts of power and replacing them with acts of love. Our unique mission is to help children and adults learn how to deal with their anger and express it in safe, constructive ways. Our philosophy is that changing our world is possible when adults approach children's misbehavior with love and compassion and teach them better ways to act.

Books for Children on Healthy Feelings by Lynne Namka

Available from www.angriesout.com or http://www.amazon.com/

The Mad Family Gets Their Mads Out

How to Let Go of Your Mad Baggage

The Case of the Prickly Feelings

Teaching Emotional Intelligence to Children: Fifty Fun Activities for Families and Therapists

Parents Fight! Parents Make Up! Take Good Care of Yourself!

Good Bye Ouchies and Grouchies. Hello Happy Feelings: EFT for Kids of All Ages

22236942R00097

Printed in Great Britain
by Amazon